The Italian X MAS

Stay-Behind Organisation:
The Black Prince's plans to sabotage Allied lines of communication in Italy in 1945

Bernard O'Connor

Contents Page

Foreword

I used to live near Tempsford Airfield, what was said to have been described by Hitler as 'a viper's nest', a top secret World War two airfield about halfway between Cambridge and Bedford and about 50 miles (80km) north of London. It was reported to have been designed by an illusionist to make it appear to overflying Luftwaffe pilots that it was disused. There were three runways, camouflaged to look like they were overgrown. Some farm buildings had been demolished, others had roof tiles removed and windows and doors broken but the inside, reinforced against bomb damage, was where RAF officers planned missions to occupied Western Europe. On the nights on either side of the full moon, after dark, planes would be taxied out of camouflaged hangars and packed with containers of arms, ammunition, explosives, sabotage material and more. Flying without lights to avoid attracting enemy night fliers, the navigator used the reflection of the moon to guide the pilot to the drop zone. Smaller planes were used to land trained secret agents in remote areas of France and Belgium and pick up passengers who the War Office and the intelligence agencies needed bringing back to Britain. Sometimes the agents were met by a reception committee, sometimes they went 'blind' and had to make their own way to a safe house or rendezvous with someone in the resistance.

Having researched and published a number of books about the airfield and the women agents who were flown from there, and other airfields, I went on to research Brickendonbury Manor, Britain's industrial sabotage school and then the activities of its graduates in Norway, Denmark, Holland, Belgium, France, Greece, the Balkans and Iberia.

The Discovery page of the National Archives' website enabled me to locate copies of folders deposited at the end of the war by British Intelligence Services. Military Intelligence Section 5 was responsible for Britain's domestic security. The Secret Intelligence Service (SIS), better known today as MI6, were responsible for the security of British interests overseas. Based in British Embassies and Consulates, SIS officers were engaged in overt and covert intelligence gathering of military, economic, political and social information which was collated and presented as reports to the

4

Foreign Minister and, in times of war, the War Office. SIS also set up D Section, sometimes referred to as the Sabotage Section, which was engaged in unsuccessful attempts to block Middle Eastern oil supplies reaching Germany via the Danube.

Following the evacuation of British diplomatic staff when German troops overtook Western Europe, SIS needed foreign-language speakers willing to be sent back covertly, often with carrier pigeons or a heavy wireless set, to undertake clandestine missions and report back.

With Britain facing invasion, members of the military community persuaded Winston Churchill, the British Prime Minister, that Britain needed a subversive intelligence agency. In July 1940, the Special Operations Executive was formed 'to set Europe ablaze by sabotage". SOE took over the work of SIS's D Section and its Propaganda Section. SOE officers, like SIS, had their own country sections. They took over the development of new weapons and wireless equipment; they requisitioned properties, trained, briefed and supplied agents with identity cards, passes, ration cards and money. They accumulated, packaged and parachuted supplies for resistance groups in enemy occupied territory. They infiltrated agents by plane, fast motor boat, fishing boat or submarine and arranged pick-ups for agents who had completed their missions. They also liaised with MI9, the section responsible for helping prisoners of war to escape and return to Britain, SIS and allied intelligence services, especially the American Office of Strategic Services (OSS).

The Field Security Section (FSS) was responsible for escorting agents during their training and to and occasionally from the airfield or port of departure.. They also defended the requisitioned properties where agents were trained, where weapons and wireless technology were being developed, and, when the Allies invaded North Africa, Italy and Western Europe. their officers were attached to the British Expeditionary Forces. Part of their responsibility included the interrogation of captured enemy personnel. Their interrogation reports were filed and deposited in the National Archives after the war.

As most of the German-trained agents infiltrated into Britain in the early stages of the war were captured or handed themselves in to the police, I was able to access their interrogation reports. From these I learned about the Abwehr, Germany's Military

Intelligence Agency, their officers, sabotage training, the schools, the syllabus, the equipment, their students and methods of infiltration, wireless communication and their missions.

During my research, I read through many reports of captured Gestapo and Abwehr officers, their trained saboteurs and collaborators who were not destined for Britain, and even enemy troops and deserters. I learned that towards the end of 1943, following the Italian Armistice and the westward advance of the Soviet Union's red Army, the Germans started preparing for their departure from occupied countries. Pro-Nazi collaborators in Spain, Italy, Greece, France, Belgium, Holland, Denmark and Norway were sent to special sabotage training schools in France, Holland, Italy and Germany. Some were trained in wireless telegraphy. In what was called 'Operation Easter Egg' caches of explosives, weapons, ammunition and sabotage material were buried and details of the locations issued to the leaders of stay-behind organisations. Once the Allies advanced through their country, these organisations were to locate the fuel pipelines, stores and main lines of tele-communication, retrieve the caches and use the contents to blow them up.

Between 2023 and 2024 I published a five-volume account of Hitler's R-Netz, resistance groups specially trained for stay-behind operations. Volume IV focussed on Italy and Volume V focussed specifically on the 'Rome Sabotage Ring.' I then moved on to research the successes and failures of Decima Flottiglia MAS, often referred to as X MAS between 1940 and the Italian surrender. X MAS was Italy's naval sabotage section headed by Prince Valerio Borghese.

As other Italian historians have covered what happened to X MAS after the September 1943 Armistice, I embarked on another project - the Allied Intelligence Services and the Vatican. Thanks to Trevor Baker, he identified many files in the National Archives which mention the Vatican, one of which was a War Office file entitled X MAS Stay Behind Organisation. This sparked the current investigation.

Thanks to Nicoletta Maggi, an Italian journalist who I collaborated with in the publication of a book on Britain's infiltration of two Soviet trained Italians into Italy in 1943, she translated some of the Italian X MAS interrogation reports. Julian

Coleman helped with the history of Villa d'Este's club house on Lake Montorfano, used by X MAS.

This book, another documentary history, tells the stories of Italian members of X MAS and the British and American officers who succeeded in arresting and interrogating them, thereby reducing the threats to Allied lines of communication and reducing Borghese's post-war political ambitions.

I need to thank the staff of the National Archives in Kew for creating the Discovery page on their website which allows visitors to locate relevant files. They kindly provided them when ordered in the reading room. I must acknowledge the help provided by Steven Kippax, the SOE historian who set up an online SOE network and made available most of the relevant files. Fred Judge, ex-archivist of the Military Intelligence Museum at Chicksands, Bedfordshire, helped Steven Kippax compile an SOE register and lists of the symbols and abbreviations used by the wartime intelligence services. As most of the SOE personnel used symbols to avoid revealing their real identities, these lists have proved invaluable.

What follows is based on the correspondence found in two X MAS files - telegrams, letters, memoranda and interrogation reports. Some documents have been redacted. As they contain names of officers who were employed after the war by the British intelligence services, MI6 and MI5, these organisations do not want their staff identified. Sometimes, governments want wartime activities to be kept secret.

Some messages were enciphered before being transmitted and then deciphered when received. Text like 'Gr. Mut.' or 'Gp. Undec.' means the group of coded letters were mutilated and therefore undecipherable. They can be explained by atmospheric disturbance or telegraphist error. Text in brackets appears in the documents. Text in square brackets is mine.

Any errors, additional information or photographs can be forwarded to the author for inclusion in a subsequent edition.

Bernard O'Connor: fquirk202@aol.com

The First Flottiglia MAS, Regia Marina's special operations assault unit – renamed Decima Flottiglia MAS in March 1941

In the mid-1930s, aware that a war with Britain was likely, a group of Italian naval officers planned to use unconventional methods to undermine the British Royal Navy's dominance of what the Romans called 'Mare Nostrum' - the Mediterranean.

In 1939 the Regia Marina, Italy's Royal Navy, set up the 1st Flottiglia Mezzi d'Assalto ("First Assault Vehicle Flotilla") headed by Capitano di Fregata (Commander) Paolo Aloisi. The MAS was an abbreviation of motoscafo armato silurante (torpedo-armed motorboat). In September 1940, a special operations section was set up, commanded by Vittorio Moccagatta. Its students, as well as studying in La Spezia, the port on the Ligurian coast, also trained in a diving school set up in the Royal Naval College in San Leopoldo, Livorno, and a camp at Bocca di Serchio, near Pisa.

After several unsuccessful operations against Allied shipping in Alexandria, on 15 March 1941 Moccagatta changed the unit's name to Decima Flottiglia MAS, sometimes written as X Flottiglia MAS or X MAS. The reason for it being called Decima has been suggested because Julius Caesar's favourite legion was Legio X Gemina. It had two sections – surface and sub-surface. The surface group, commanded by Ernesto Forza, operated fast explosive motorboats. The sub-surface group, commanded by Borghese, used human-guided torpedoes and included 'Gamma" assault swimmers (nuotatori) who used magnetic limpet mines to blow up underwater targets. (https://en.wikipedia.org/wiki/Decima_Flottiglia_MAS; https://en.wikipedia.org/wiki/Vittorio_Mocca gatta)

Between September 1940 and August 1943, teams of Italian 'frogmen' attacked Allied shipping in Malta, Corfu, Gibraltar and Spain and Turkey. The X MAS sent 238 men in 38 separate missions. Of these, 20 died in action, and 53 were taken prisoners. They sank or damaged five warships totalling 78,000 tons and 20 merchant ships totalling 130,000 tons. (https://comandosupremo.com/decima-mas/)

Those who were taken into custody by the British were interrogated by Counter-Intelligence officers about their organisation, their training schools, their syllabus, the officers, other students and their missions. Their interrogation reports, deposited in the National Archives in Kew, allowed me to write *'Italy's Mediterranean Sea Devils: Decima Flottiglia MAS 1940 – 1943'*.

Following the Allied invasion of Sicily on 9 July 1943, the Fascist Grand Council voted Mussolini out of office on 25 July. On 3 September, Allied troops landed at Salerno and, with the agreement of King Victor Emmanuel III and Marshal Pietro Badoglio, the Prime Minister, an armistice was signed. On 9 September, Italy surrendered unconditionally to the Allies.

The German response, Operation Achse, was to attack Italian forces in Northern Italy, Southern France and the Balkans. Italian soldiers were disarmed and imprisoned to prevent them being used by the Allies. They also established a series of defensive lines running from the Adriatic to the Tyrrhenian Sea to deter the Allies advancing north. Mussolini was freed and the Repubblica Sociale Italiana (Italian Social Republic - RSI) was established with him as its leader. The Italian King, the Italian government and most of the Italian Navy fled to Southern Italy where they were under the protection of the Allies. A resistance or partisan movement was formed, supplied by the Allies with British and American agents co-ordinating them.

Some of the X MAS men in southern Italy and other Allied-occupied areas were loyal to the King. Admiral Aimone de Savoia, Commandant of X MAS, Forza and other royalists captured by the Allies were released from prisoner of war camps to serve in the Italian Co-Belligerent Navy as part of the Mariassalto (Naval Assault) unit. This unit is referred to later.

In Northern and Central Italy disorder in the Army and Navy spread. In La Spezia, stores, arsenals and headquarters were abandoned to lotting and destruction. Borghese resisted German attempts to infiltrate and loot government property. 400 X MAS personnel were given indefinite leave except for nine men he kept with him. Once SS Otto Skorzeny and his team had freed Mussolini from house arrest, and the RSI had been established, Borghese deciding to continue to support the Germans in their fight against the Allies. He recalled former X MAS personnel and recruited others from the military to form an anti-partisan special forces unit which targeted communist groups in Northern Italy. By November 1943 he had about 1,000 and by the end of the war CSDIC estimated the number as between 50,000 and 60,000. However, some were subsequently accused of war crimes including torture, sexual abuse and virtual enslavement of Italian youths near Marzabotto in 1944. Others volunteered as stay-behind saboteurs, espionage agents and wireless operators. (https://historica.fandom.com/wiki/Decima_Flottiglia_MAS#: ~:text=Decima%20Flottiglia%20Mezzi%20d'Asalto,1943%20dur ing%20World%20War%20 II; https://en.wikipedia.org/wiki/ Decima_Flottiglia_MAS; TNA WO204/12803)

Prince Valerio Borghese, Commander of the 10 Flotilla MAS
(Borghese, Valerio, *Sea Devils,* Andrew Melrose, 1952)

Valerio Borghese took command of Decima Flottiglia MAS in 1942 (https://www.warhistoryonline.com/instant-articles/scire-italian-royal-navy-sub.html)

Valerio Borghese, Commander of the 10th MAS Flotilla (https://preview.redd.it/yrljg9ak2vxy.jpg?width=1080&crop =smart&auto=webp&s=23a534095c9b2ce3ed9d24bd5e1a9fc 3fba1bed9)

SCI/UNIT Z/U.S.
1 Piazza Strozzi,
Florence.

Memo No. 347

8 March 1945

SUBJECT: Enemy Sabotage Agents.

TO: AC of S, (Ib), G-2, 15th Army Group.

1. The following message was received this date from one of our OSS field teams:

"SOURCE INFORMS ON 1 MARCH THAT THE COMMAND OF THE TENTH MAS OF MILANO IS PREPARING A MISSION TO SABOTAGE AN ALLIED OIL PIPE LINE WHICH IS IN THE VICINITY OF FLORENCE. THE DE-PARTURE OF A SMALL GROUP OF MILITIA MEN, PROVIDED WITH FORGED DOCUMENTS, IS IMMINENT."

2. Further details will be submitted immediately upon receipt.

PAUL J. PATERNI,
1st Lt., AUS,
Commanding SCI/Z/FLORENCE.

CC:

AC of S, (CI), G-2, 5th Army
GSI (b) Main 8th Army
#3 SCI/Florence
SCI/Z/Rome
File

(TNA WO202/13000)

12

The X MAS Stay-behind organisation

The Italian Armistice was followed by the westward advance of the Soviet Union's Red Army which forced German troops to retreat. Some in the German High Command planned for a withdrawal from other occupied countries. Pro-Nazi collaborators in Spain, France, Belgium, Holland, Denmark, Norway Greece and Italy were sent to special sabotage training schools in France, Holland, Germany and Northern Italy. Some were trained in wireless telegraphy.

In what the Abwehr, Germany's military intelligence service, called 'Operation Easter Egg', caches of explosives, weapons, ammunition and sabotage material were buried and details of the locations issued to the leaders of stay-behind organisations. Once the Allies advanced through their country, these organisations were to locate the fuel pipelines, stores and main lines of tele-communication, retrieve the caches and use the contents to blow them up.

Volume IV of *Destroying Hitler's R-Netz* details the Abwehr's stay-behind organisation in Italy. Volume V investigates the Rome Sabotage Ring. This book investigates the X MAS stay-behind organisation during 1944 and 1945.

When the Germans took over Northern Italy in September 1943, the Hotel Villa d'Este on the banks of Lake Como, was requisitioned for SS Hauptsturmführer Joseph Voetterl of the Frontier Guards, who were attempting to halt the crossing of the border into Switzerland by escaped prisoners of war and Jews. Research by British historian Julian Copeland revealed that the hotel also had a golf course and club house on the shore of Lake Montorfano, about 3 miles (4.8km) south of Como and 25 miles (40km) north of Milan. X MAS occupied the club house as their headquarters. (https://comocompanion.com/)

Whether X MAS documents relating to the period 1944 – 45 survived the war is unknown. What is also not known is whether the Germans were behind the X MAS stay-behind groups or they were Borghese's idea. What is known is that some of the X MAS personnel trained for stay-behind operations were captured by Allied troops and interrogated. Their reports help shed light on

Recent photograph of Villa d'Este, Lake Montorfano,
headquarters of X MAS Flotilla 1944-45
(https://comocompanion.com/2020/04/27/comos-lake-
montorfano-commandos-contraband-and-the-cia/)

In the weeks before the Allies entered Rome, American troops
apprehended a number of Italians at check points attempting to
cross the lines into Allied Occupied Territory (AOT). Assisted by

14

Italian carabinieri, everyone was checked at road blocks, bus stations, train stations, ferry ports, airports and border crossings to see whether they had appropriate travel passes or their names were on a list of wanted Fascists and German personnel. Those identified by the British as potential threats were taken to a Combined Services Detailed Interrogation Centre (CSDIC). Those identified by the Americans were sent to a Special Counter-Intelligence Unit, temporary accommodation which moved as the Allies advanced north. Both were attached to Army Groups and were in communication via telephone, telegram and courier.

As well as being thoroughly searched, people who were stopped had to answer questions about their birth, their family, their education and their military history were checked to see whether they corresponded to their identity papers, passes and other intelligence the Allies might have had on them. A filing system of postcard-sized notes able to be cross-checked was built up. Those on the wanted list or identified as suspicious were photographed, had forms filled in and, after interrogation, reports typed up and copies sent to the relevant security sections in the hope that they would be apprehended.

January 1945

One of the War Office files in the National Archives is entitled 'Longone Sabotage School'. Amongst its students were men from X MAS. Longone al Segrino is a small village and commune between Como and Lecco in the province of Como in Lombardy, Italy. It is located about 40 kilometres north of Milan and about 13 kilometres east of Como. From the sketch map in the file it appears that the school was in a hotel 14 Via Vittoria Emmanuelle.

The first document contains a note written at the top stating that it was an 'Abstract from interrogation report of PISCIA Federico CSDIC/CMF/Z.123 of 22 Jan 45. It was written by Major R. N. Bridge, the Commanding Officer of Counter Intelligence Section, CSDIC, CMF.

A.   LOCATIONS

I. FIDE Group (FP No 17349)

MILAN	5, Plazza CADORNA, REME's office (12 Oct 44) Albergo MALTECCA. Used by PRACHT for interviewing agents (Oct 44)
CAMPAGNOLA	Shop in square owned by chemist named BIGI (?) Subject signed his undertaking to the group here.
NOGARA	Albergo ? Requisitioned for FIDE Group on 29 Oct 44. Before that used for billeting agents.

For location and plan of this hotel and other agents billets used in Oct 44, see Appendices "B", "C" and "D".
[Nogara is a commune in the Province of Verona in the Italian region of Veneto, located about 100 kilometres southwest of Venice and about 30 kilometres south of Verona.]

REGGIO-EMILIA	Albergo DIURNO Residence of agents (as at 10 Oct 44)

II Sonder kdo MAGNUS (FP No 40010
LONGONE (Prov COMO)   Villa BELDOSSO
Sabotage School (Ref Map ITALY 1:25,000 Sheet 32 MR
E316024

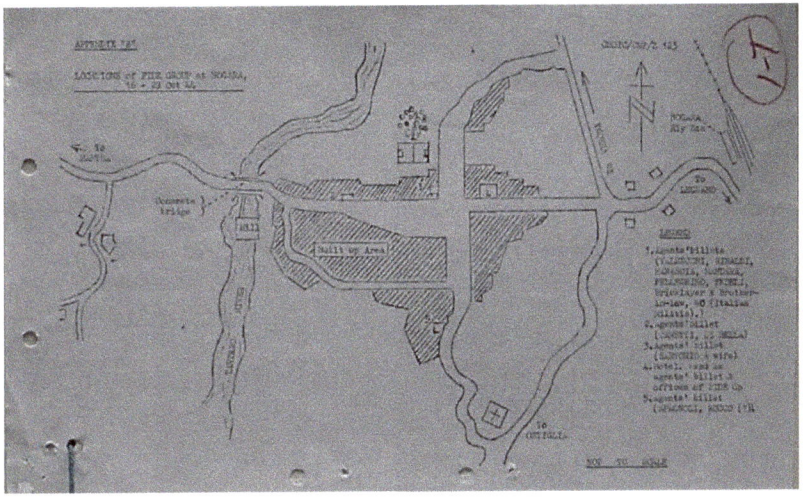

Possible location of Nogara Sabotage school, 14 Via Vittoria Emmanuelle

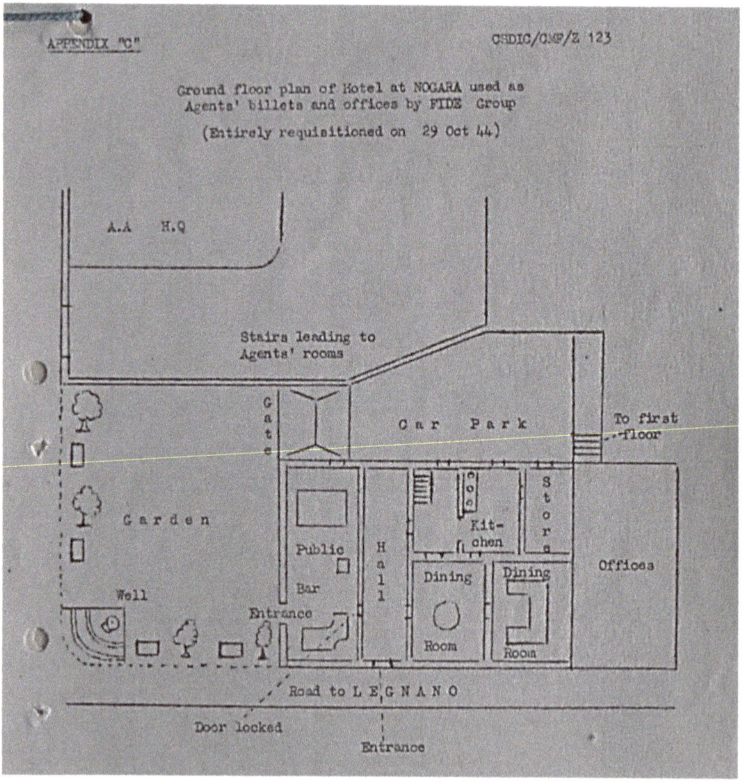

APPENDIX "C"   CSDIC/CMF/Z 123

Ground floor plan of Hotel at NOGARA used as
Agents' billets and offices by FIDE Group

(Entirely requisitioned on 29 Oct 44)

A.A H.Q

Stairs leading to
Agents' rooms

Gate

Car Park   To first
                            floor

Garden

Public   Kit-   Store
                chen
Well   Bar   Hall Dining Dining   Offices

Entrance

Room   Room

Road to L E G N A N O

Door locked   Entrance

18

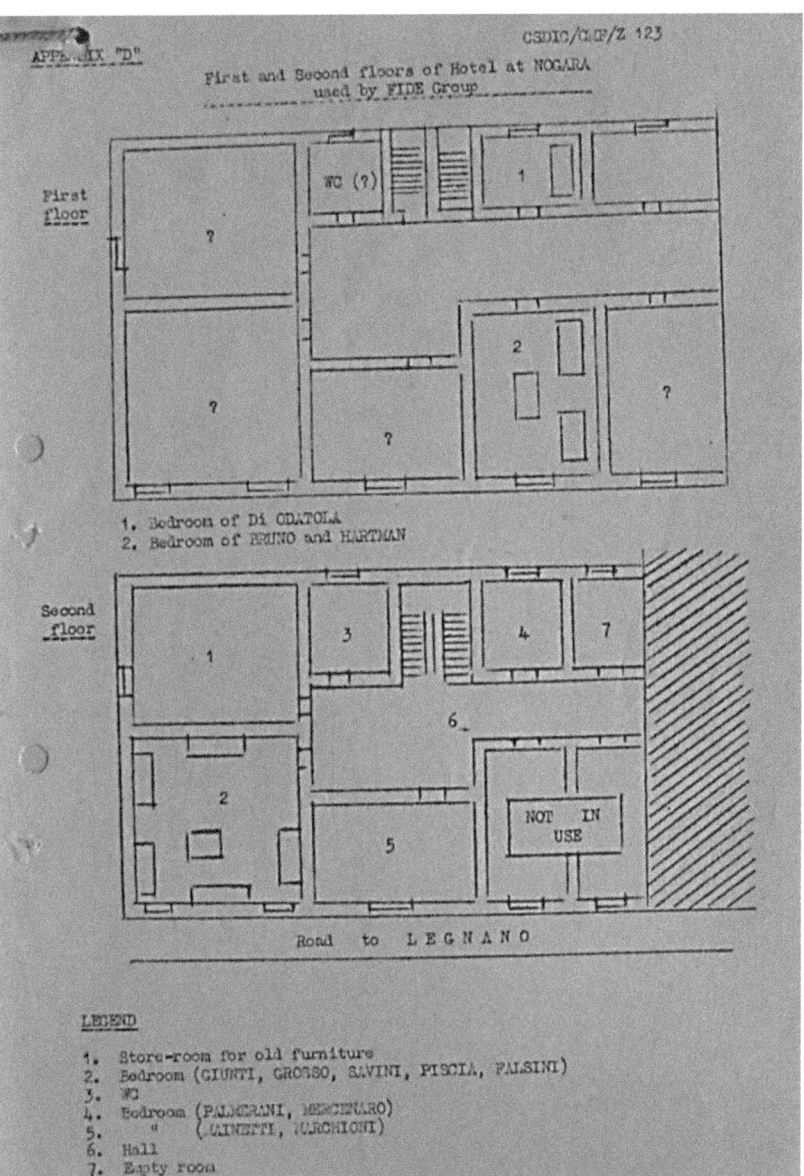

First and Second floors of Hotel at NOGARA
used by FIDE Group

First
floor

WC (?)

1

?

?

2

?

?

1. Bedroom of Di ODATOLA
2. Bedroom of BRUNO and HARTMAN

Second
floor

1

3

4

7

6

2

5

NOT IN
USE

Road   to   L E G N A N O

LEGEND

1. Store-room for old furniture
2. Bedroom (GIURTI, GROSSO, SAVINI, PISCIA, FALSINI)
3. WC
4. Bedroom (PALMERINI, MERCINARO)
5.   "   (MAINETTI, MARCHIONI)
6. Hall
7. Empty room

(TNA WO204/12419)

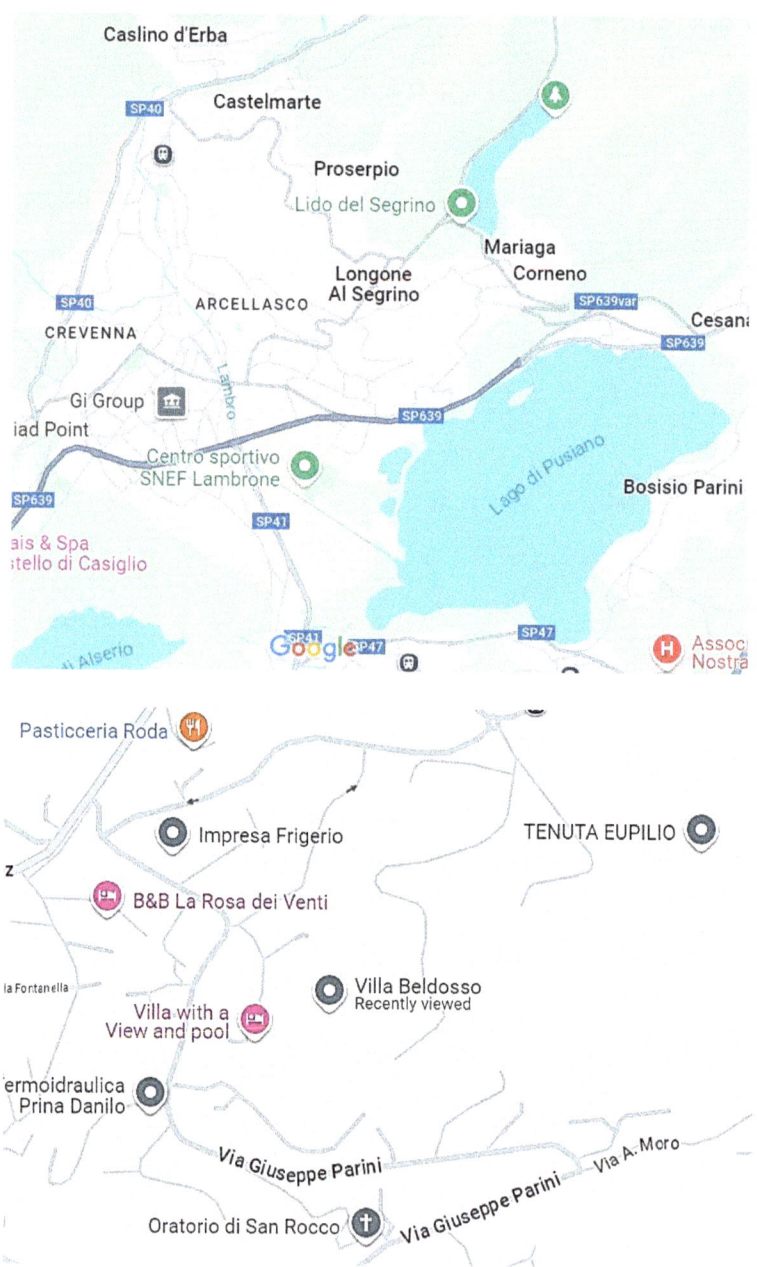

Early postcard of Villa Beldosso, Longone, Sabotage School
from October 1944
(https://i.ebayimg.com/images/g/6ZAAAOSwpqhhfHHF/s
-l1600.webp)

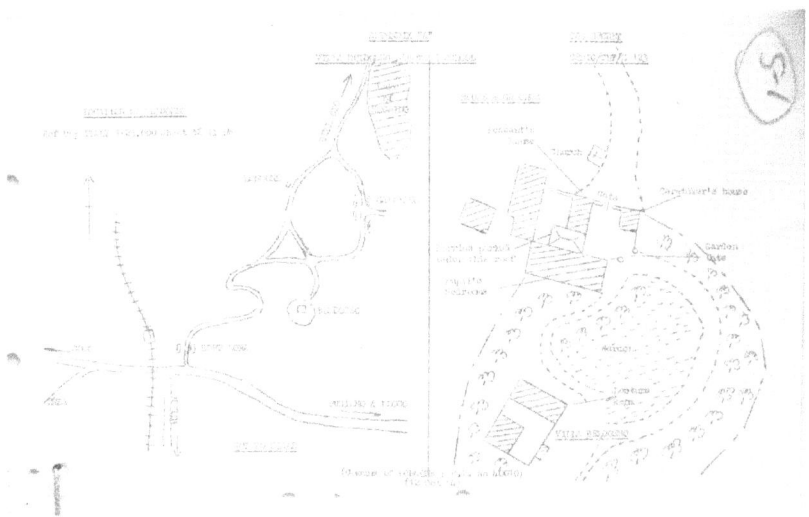

B. ORGANISATION

I. FIDE Group (Sep – early Nov 44)a) Personnel seen
    by Subject in or connected with the Group (all in List
    C)
    Capt TODISCO (possibly MUELLER)

Lieut KLAUSEN
Lieut WAGNER
Lieut NIMIC
REME
German (officer?) seen once at Albergo
MALTECCA, MILAN.
German WO [Warrant Officer]
Sgt HARTMANN Otello (Instructor)
Cpl PRACHT (Interviewer)
Cpl "Albert" (Interpreter)
Cpl "Rudolf" (Driver)
"Bruno"   (Interpreter)
Pte "Charles" (Driver)
Pte ? (Driver)
Pte ? (Driver)
Sgt RAVENNI (recruited for 10 Flotilla MAS)

b) Method of Recruitment from 10 Flotilla MAS

RAVENNI, while still receiving pay from the 10 Flotilla to
which he belonged, was paid by the Group to recruit agents
from the Flotilla – for this he received normal agent's pay of
200 lire a day plus a bonus of 5000 lire for each man recruited.
At the beginning of Sep [1944] he liaised with Tenente
VERCESI, OC a Section of the NP Bn at the 10 Flotilla
Sabotage School at MONTORFANO, who said he was
willing to supply a number of men to do sabotage work for
the Germans provided they wore uniform, and the Italians
had an equal share with the Germans in the planning of
operations. This proposal was turned down by "Albert" when
RAVENSI reported it to him later.

The Group appears ton have gone to some pains to keep on
the right side of 10 Flotilla authorities. Thus PRACHT at first
wanted Subject, SAVINI and GROSS to return to their Bn
when he heard they had deserted, and when VERCESI paid a
visit to the LONGONE Sabotage School these three were
told to keep out of the way.

c) Conditions for Agents

Pay was 200 Lire a day, out of which agents were expected to
provide themselves with board and lodging, where necessary,

and clothing. A ration of ten cigarettes a day was also provided. On one occasion, in MILAN, agents were given an extra 100 lire for four days to cover the high cost of living in MILAN.

d) Security
Civilian clothes were worn at all times. Pupils at the LONGONE School were all given aliases, but most of them knew one another's real names, as post came to the School addressed normally. Though secrecy about individual missions and payment was stressed, the agents who left with Subject for the front on 10 Nov mostly knew each had been given 30,000 lire for a specific sabotage mission in Allied Occupied Territory. (For security procedure on mission, see para C. X).

e) Method of Operating.
Originally Subject was told that he would be used as a post-occupational agent. Shortly before he left on his mission, he and SAVINI were told that plans had been changed, and that the mission would be the unburying and use of explosives buried in Allied Occupied Territory. He believes the other eleven agents were given similar missions.

f) CORREGGIO Sabotage School
No details known, as, though Subject was intended for a course there in mid-Sep, this plan was changed.
Instructor at that time was HARTMANN Otello. Believed to have been disbanded for reasons given in para 54 of Narrative.

g) NOGARA Sabotage School
Subject believed a Sabotage School was being set up at NOGARA in Oct. For reasons see above mentioned para.

II. Villa BELDOSSO Sabotage School .(FP 40010. Also known as Sonder-Kommando MAGNUS)
a) Personnel
Capt KLEIN (OC)
MARTIN (OC Course)

Sgt MUELLER Hans (Instructor)
Mr DEDESCHEK (Interpreter)
Warrant Officer
Sgt SCHILLIKAU (i/c Quartermaster's and weapon store
Sgt SCHIERRER (Administration)
Col Fritz(Odd jobs)
Pte PEER (Odd jobs)
Pte REINCKE (Capt KLEIN's driver)
Pte TITZ (Cook)
Pte SHIATOWSKI (Odd jobs)

b) Disbandment

All equipment and effects had been taken to ERBA station for delivery elsewhere (rumoured TRENTO) as at 12 Oct 44, as the School was being disbanded. Pupils were told that the new school would contrive to carry the same FP No as before (i.e. 40010). Subject believed that the premises were being taken over by Italian SS troops.

METHODS

Premises

The School was located in a large Villa situated in its own grounds a mile or so from LONGONE (MR ITALY 1:25000 – E316024). Pupils were quartered in another building in the grounds (See map Appendix "A".

Pupils

(X – Pupils who have been sent across the lines and have already been arrested)
X PISCIA Federico (Subject)
X SAVINI Ettore
X GROSSO Luciano
X FALSINI Ugo
X GIUNTI Carlo
X MARCHIONI Pepino
X MAINETTI Pepino
   CANETTI Giulio
   Capt DI BELLA
X VALSECCHI Ugo

24

X RINALDI Giorgio
X FABBI Aristide
X MARASCIA Emilio
X MANDARA Antonio
X PELLEGRINO Ubaldo
X FEDELI Gigi
  SPAGNOLI Ivo
  ROCCO
  Lieut SARTORIO Rino
  Signora SARTORIO (wife of above)
  A bricklayer (name unknown)
  Brother-in-law of above
  A WO [Warrant Officer] of the Militia

III. Specimen Day's Programme

Reveille	0630 hrs
Breakfast	0700 – 0800 hrs
Course	0800 – 1100
Lunch and Rest	1200 – 1500
Course	1500 – 1730
Dinner	1800

IV. Devices Taught

1. Explosives
   a) Solid "TRINI" (TRITOL) in rectangular cubes of 1 kg wrapped in metal cover, ½ kg wrapped in dark blue paper, and ¼ kg wrapped in yellow paper.
   b) Plastic in cylinders of 200 gr each wrapped in a yellow paper with "PE NO 2" printed on.
   c) Industrial Explosives A greyish powder in packets of 250 gr wrapped in yellow paper. This was used at the school to save Plastic and Tritol.

2. Ignition Devices
   a) Primer for industrial purposes and Plastic in large quantities. To be used together with detonator. 6cm long and 2 cm in diameter cardboard tube with a small hole on flat surface to introduced the detonator. Colour yellow, top

was either red, green or white, but Subject was told these colours had special meaning.

b) Detonators.

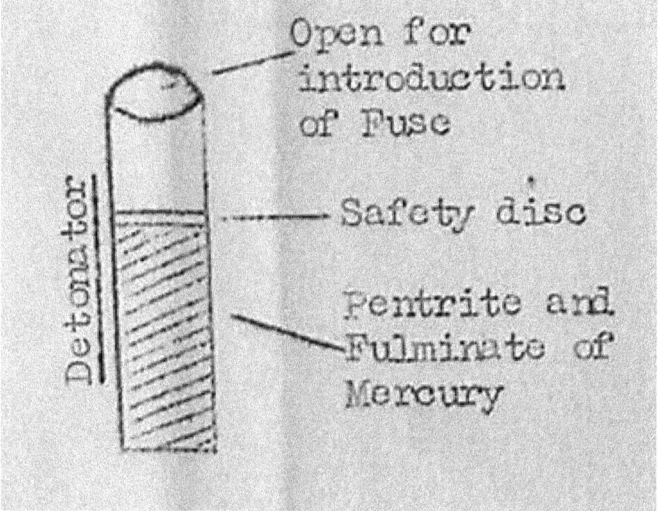

British, German and Italian. All alike in shape. British were more dangerous to handle because of lack of safety device . Aluminium tube 5 cm long, ½ cm in diameter. Contains Pentrite and Fulminate of Mercury. German and Italian detonators have a small disc with a hole in the centre which prevents the fuse from touching the explosive substance.

c. Detonator Tipo "S" to use with time pencil

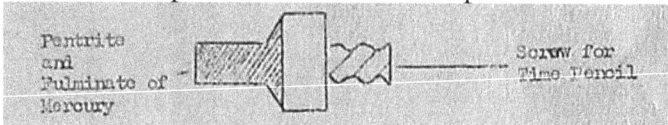

d. Fuses

i) Time fuse containing black powder. Burns at the speed of 1 cm per second. The fuse is either white or black.

ii) Detonating fuse containing Pentrite. Burns at the speed of 6 to 7 cms per second. German fuse is given with red thread at centre, Italian is black with red thread in spiral round it.

e. Matches. British made which produce only heat and no flame and cannot be seen burning at night.

f. Time Pencils
i. Normal type (see War Office Publication Fig. 3 & 4)
ii. Ii. Special. Lead tube 15 cms long. 1 cm in diameter.

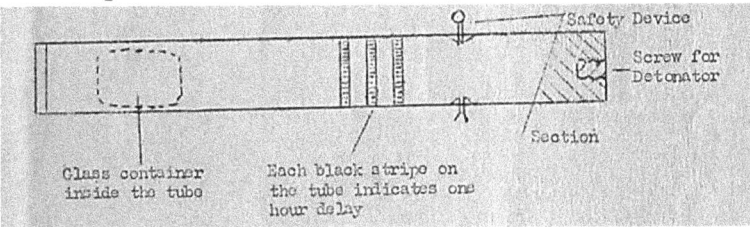

g. Igniters
i) Fuse Igniter

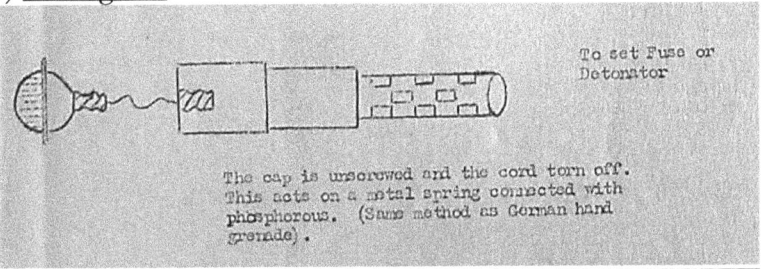

ii) Electric Igniter

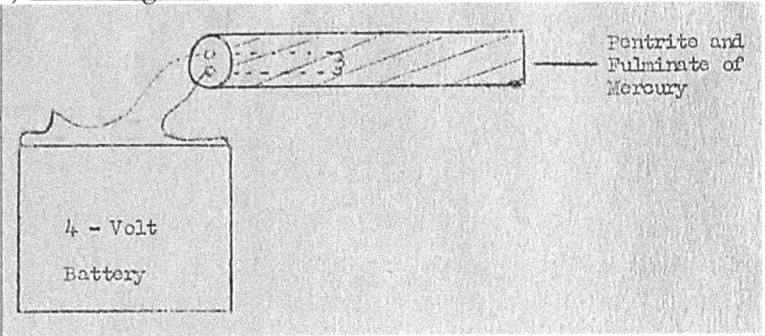

iii) Igniters for Railways
See Fig 3 page A4 AFHQ Publication "Sabotage Devices".
iv) Incendiary Igniter
Can only be used with time fuse or time pencil. Coloured red to distinguish them from the others. The incendiary igniter produces a small flame whereas the ordinary detonator does not and cannot therefore be used for incendiaries.
3. Incendiaries

a) <u>Cardboard Box</u> 10 cms high and 10 cms in diameter containing phosphorous and thermite. Buring time: 4 minutes. Weight: 1 Kg. Develops a very high temperature, approx.. 2500°C. Ejects small pieces of red hot metal. This device must be ignited with the incendiary igniter (the normal detonator does not work).

b) <u>Black Cylinder</u> as shown at Fig. 13, page 11 War Office Publication.

i) Type A 20 cms long 5 cms in diameter weight 1 Kg

ii) Type B 10 cms   2½ cms   ½ Kg

The fuse passes through the top and can be pulled out on one side or the other. To set to a given delay cut a nick at sufficient distance from one end to allow delay required. Pull through from other end to allow nick to come opposite the top of the cylinder.

iii)   <u>Incendiary Celluloid Box</u> 12 cms in diameter and 2 cms high with yellow phosphor on one side (to light). Contents: paraffin and resin. Burning time: 14 to 15 minutes. The flame produced is smoky, red and low. Not very high temperature. Used for clothing stores, paper stores etc.

4.   <u>Hand Grenade</u>

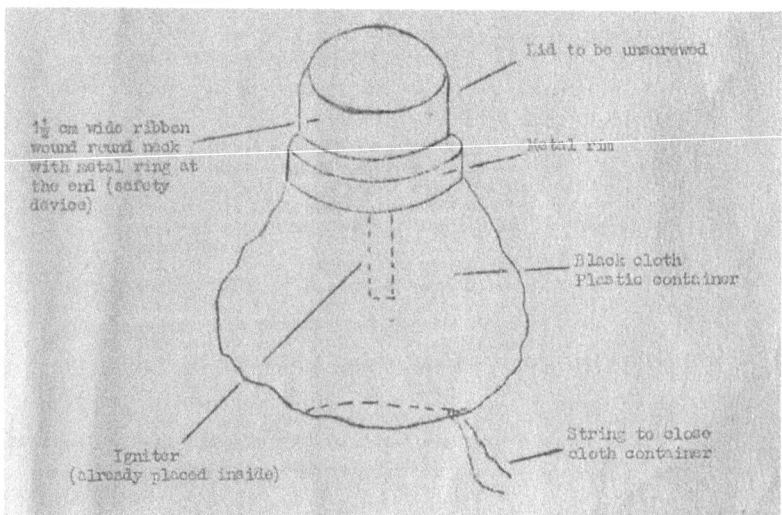

The plastic [explosive] is placed inside a black cloth container with the the strings are tightened. The cap is unscrewed and the grenade is thrown making sure that the ribbon round the neck is unwound. The weight of the metal ring at the end of the tape will make it fall off (if it does not fall off the grenade does not explode). The grenade will explode as soon as it hits the ground.

5. Explosive Charcoal

Is mostly used to throw in a railway tender among the coal.

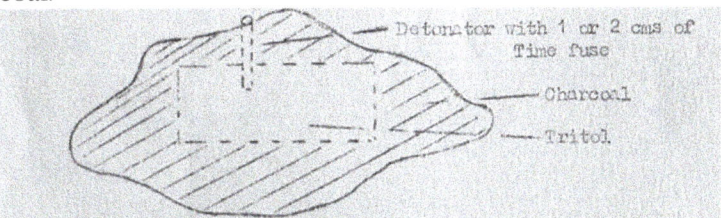

Fuse will be set by the fire in the furnace of the engine.

6. Micromines

To be places on roads or at entrance of soldiers' canteens and clubs.

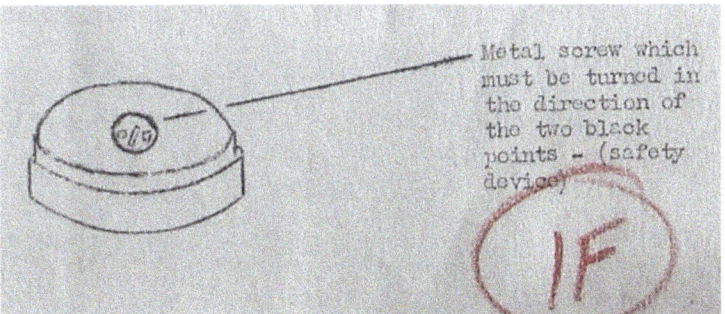

7. Magnets to hold Plastic of Solid explosives against metal

Objectives

The use of highly concentrated explosive (not expanded) was advised. Two types of magnets are in use: small and large.

For 2Kgs of explosives use 4 large magnets

     2 Kgs   6 small

Small magnets were said to be more advisable, as the explosive remains more compact than with the large, but if a large hole had to be cut in a thin piece of metal the use of large magnets was recommended. If on the contrary a small hole had to be blasted in the same thickness of metal, then the use of small magnets was recommended. The Plastic or Tritol is placed in a cardboard box, with the magnets being on top. Holes are drilled in the lid of the box, so that each magnet faces a hole, and is sucked through when applied against a metal surface. (Subject was told never to use Plastic or Tritol with magnets without using the box).

Applications: Tanker waggons and tanker trucks, petrol tanks in dumps.

The use of magnets is advised when the saboteur has to work very rapidly. The charge should always be placed underneath the waggon or the truck to reduce the chances of falling off.

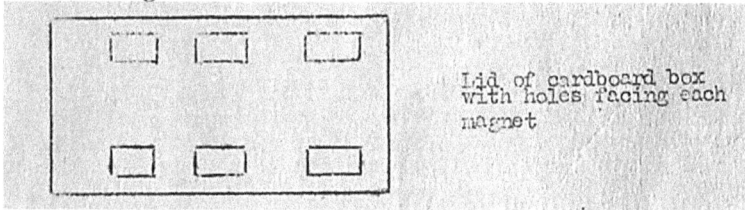

Lid of cardboard box with holes facing each magnet

V.   Formulae

The formulae taught were very simple and though slightly in excess of the quantities required, pupils were advised to use them as they were easy to remember.

1.   Tritol
   a)   Wood   1 gr of Tritol per sq cm of cross section
   b)   Iron   25gr
   c)   Concrete   50gr

2.   Plastic
   Half the quantities specified above.

VI. Methods Taught

1.   Sabotage with Explosives and Incendiaries

30

a) <u>On railway trucks</u> the explosive should be fired above the attachments of the springs (between the spring and the body of the truck), or on the hooks that link trucks together.

b) <u>On railway trucks containing goods</u> 400 gr of plastic applied with magnets, plus one incendiary bomb with two fuses. To be applied on lower part of truck.

c) <u>On tanker waggon</u> the same devices should be places behind the metal boards indicating the destination of the truck. If no incendiary material is available, then apply explosive on top of the tank where a layer of gas exists, which will help to set the petrol on fire.

d) <u>On open trucks</u> loaded with clothing or paper; if one can get away quickly, through a celluloid incendiary box. Otherwise the 1 Kg cardboard box with time pencil.

e) <u>On open railway trucks loaded with lorries, tanks, or guns</u> Place a small charge of explosive which will destroy the cables and boards fixing the load on the railway truck. The movement of the train will do the rest. A quick method as the saboteur does not have to climb on the truck.

f) <u>On locomotives</u>
   i)   Application of explosive on the connecting rods (between the wheels)
   ii) Explosive charcoal thrown in the tender.

g) <u>Railway truck</u>
   This should always be attacked in tunnels, on curves, or in a cutting, in order to make repair work more difficult.

h) <u>First Method</u> Place the charges of 400 gr of plastic each on either side of the fish plate on the outer side of each rail. Also place a railway detonator on the rail after the second charge of plastic and one detonator in the first. Connect detonator on the rail to the three detonators in the plastic with detonating fuse. If detonators are not available to place inside the plastic one knot should be made in the detonating fuse for each detonator not available and inserted in the hole in which the detonator would have been introduced.

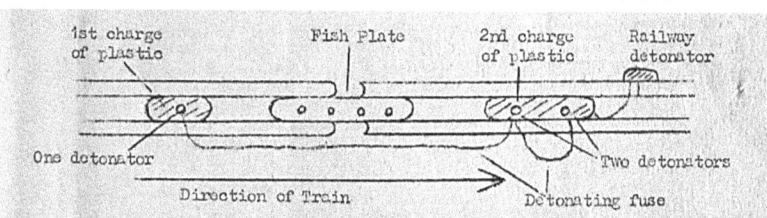

The charges of plastic should be camouflaged with sand, leaves or stones.

ii) Second Method (with electric igniter)

Place the two charges of 400 gr of plastic as above. Instead of using the railway detonator on top of rail use one electric igniter in charge No. 2. Connect first wire on the igniter to position pole on 4-volt battery, and second wire on the rail. The negative pole of the battery should be wrapped in insulating tape and place on the rail. (The weight of the wheels would destroy the tape and create the necessary contact). All the other connections are the same as for method 1, i.e. detonating fuse connecting other detonators, or if detonators are not available, knots tied in detonating fuse and inserted in holes in plastic.

iii)   Third Method

Same as above with time fuse and time pencil. This is only possible if the area is not properly guarded and the saboteur has plenty of time at his disposal.

h)   On Points and Railway Crossings

i) 800 gr of plastic in the centre of the points or at the point where the rails cross. Same method as above with railway detonator or time pencil.

ii) In the case of points called "scambio inglese" place two charges of 800 gr each at each point.

i) Turntables for locomotives and Waggons

The charge should be set in the gear wheel. The quantity varies according to the size and cross section.

j) Water Towers in Stations

Damage the water pipe (exit of water); the higher the pressure the greater the damage. If more than one oner tower exists in the station try and damage them all so as to leave the station without water.

k) Control Cabins

Damage the control wires so as to disrupt signals and disorganise train traffic.

l) Goods Stores in Stations

The saboteur will have to choose whether he is going to use explosives or incendiaries according to the goods that are being attacked. In the case of ammunition or explosives a very small charge of plastic with time pencil is sufficient. In the case of petrol tanks a charge of explosive on the upper part of the tank, or of explosive and incendiary on the lower part. If a petrol dump is situated in a valley the saboteur must not light a match, but place a time pencil and escape to higher ground, as there are gas fumes down in the valley.

m) Motor Vehicles

For destroying or damaging the vehicle itself, the most vulnerable points are the springs, the front axle and the rear axle, or the petrol tanks on both sides of the vehicle.

To damage front axle   400 gr of plastic

               rear axle (differential)   200 gr

               petrol tanks   Place a ring of 200 gr of plastic around the cap.

               transmission shaft   A ring of 300 gr of plastic around the shaft.

For destroying the contents of the vehicle the charges and methods vary according to the contents.

n) Power Cables

   i) Wooden Poles

     Calculate cross section of pole and place charge of plastic. Poles on a curve should be selected to cause more effective destruction.

   ii) Metal Pylons

     Place two charges on two opposite poles if the pylon is on a curve. If it is in a straight line then apply a charge on each of the four poles.

   iii) Concrete Poles

     Sabotage of these is not advised as too great a quantity of explosive is required.

o) Wooden Bridges

If the saboteur has not sufficient fuse to connect four or five charges of explosive he should place the charges in a perfectly straight line, at a distance of one metre from another if they are of 600 gr each, and 1½ m if they are of 1 Kg each. A detonator is set in each charge, slightly protruding and facing towards the adjacent detonator, this will cause sympathetic explosion of all of the charges.

p) Ammunition Dumps

A small charge of 300 to 400 gr of plastic with tiem pencil or time fuse should be set among the ammunition cases. If the dump is divided in several sections a set will be placed in each section.

2. Sabotage without Explosives

   a) Railway Waggons

     Concentrate on goods waggons.

     i) Introduce sand or iron powder and filings in the greasers of the wheels, having first removed the filter.

ii) Alter the regulator of the brake from the position in which it is found.

iii) Cut the tube of the brakes. Operate underneath the waggon so that the cut cannot be seen.

iv) If on one and the same train there are, for instance, Italian and French waggons which have two different systems of brakes, the first being Westinghouse and the second Vacuum, connect the tubes together. As one system works by increased and the second by reduced air pressure an accident is bound to occur. The Westinghouse has a plain connection at the end of the tube whereas the Vacuum has the connection painted in white with a red cross in the centre.

v) Change the destination of the truck by changing the board on the truck by erasing and re-writing in chalk.

b) Steam Locomotives

i) Introduce sand and other abrasives in the lubrication system.

ii)   Loosen the bolts on the connecting rods.

iii)   Cut the oil tubes on the brakes.

iv)   Smash the steam pressure and water level indicators. (This is a minor form of sabotage as the engine driver would notice it before stating, but it would cause a delay, of several hours at times, until the locomotive is changed.

c) Electric Locomotives

i) Sand and other abrasives in the lubricating tubes,

ii)   Acid and corrosive liquids in all the electrical parts.

iii) Damage the "controller" with acids, or possibly the engine (very effective, as this would not be notices until after the train has started).

d) Points

i) Remove link between the needles at points.

ii) Damage electrical installation at points. This is usually in a box near the points, which contains a small engine, shaft, etc. Damage can easily be done with a stone or by breaking the box with a strong kick.

iii) Changing points is too elementary according to Subject, as it shows immediately in the control cabin, when installations are electrical.

iv) In the case of points called "Tipo Inglese" sabotage is very effective because by damaging and interrupting one point the whole system is disrupted. According to the Official at MILAN Station who showed the pupils round (during a practise exercise) this type of sabotage would interrupt a line for at least a fortnight, as there are no spare parts available.

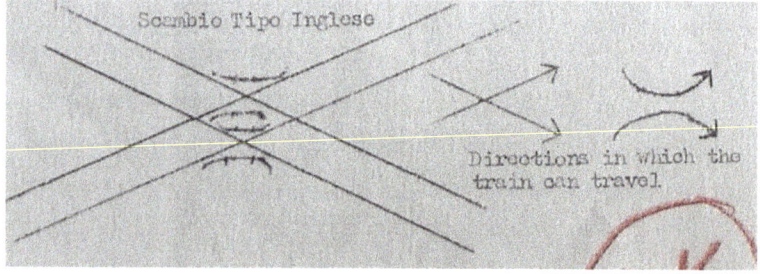

Scambio Tipo Inglese

Directions in which the train can travel

e) Signals

i) Block the signal by removing the lever (essential not to let the signal drop, as it would show in the control cabin). This is only to prevent the signal from dropping to indicate the line is clear.

ii) Cut electrical wires if signals are electrical.

iii) Change the colour glasses on signals. (This is only for night signals).

iv) Signals "Tipo Marmotte (electrical)

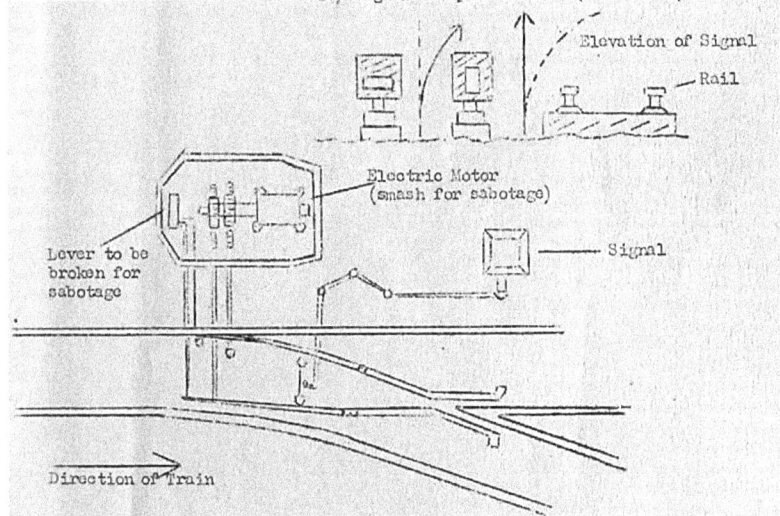

f) Control Cabins

Damage or break the point levers. In a station like MILAN Central where all the installations are electrical, this type of sabotage is very effective as it is extremely difficult to work these by hand.

g) Gear wheels

Introduce a piece or iron or any metal in the teeth and make sure that it is dragged inside (and not pushed out) as the wheel turns.

h) Motor Vehicles

i. Cut plug wires.

ii. Reverse plug wires

iii. Introduce pieces of iron or any other metal into the battery.

iv. Damage the feed pipe (from petrol tank to carburettor).

v. Break the glass petrol filter.

vi. Introduce sand and other abrasives in gear box, differential, and engine, (also nuts, screws, etc).

vii. Damage the connecting tube of fluid brakes on one side only, so that the vehicle may overturn through uneven brakage.

viii. Damage the brake connection between a lorry and trailer.

ix. Place a sharp nail in a cork and place the device near the wheel of a vehicle so as to cause a puncture. (Flat nails on the road are useless.).

VII Practical Exercises
1. Topography
   a) Copying from the blackboard (reducing the scale) very simple topographical sketches.
   b) 6 – 7 km walks across country in the neighbourhood of the Villa. As soon as the pupils returned they had to draw a sketch of the roads they had been on, and indicate all the main features, such as bridges, power stations, conspicuous buildings like chapels, etc. They also had to indicate the nature of the ground, whether woody, hilly, flat or open country.
   c) Every student had to buy an object in the surroundings of the Villa, then make a sketch of the place where the object was buried. The sketch was then given to another student who had to find the object. Later the students had to look for the object after having memorised the sketch, and finally they had to go through the same procedure by night.

2. Memory Tests and Orientation
   The students were asked what type of figures were on their watches (Roman or Arabic). Very few answered correctly.

They were also asked, while indoors, where the North was.

3. Indoor Work on Sabotage Material
    a) How to cut fuses and insert them in detonators.
    b) How to light fuses with matches, with special anti-wind matches and with cigarettes.
    c) Application of more than one fuse to one detonator. Insert time fuse in detonator, then apply first detonating fuse on detonator and attach with adhesive tape, then fold the detonating fuse and attach again. See sketch below).

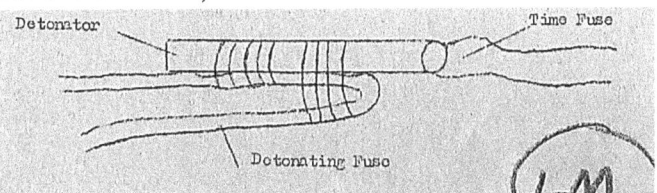

The maximum number of detonators and detonating fuses that one time fuse can support are 6 detonators and 36 detonating fuses.
(In the case of a bridge with five arches, five charges can be placed with one detonator only and five detonating fuses, each one leading to one of the charges. It is essential that the fuses should not cross, otherwise they would cut each other.).
    d) Preparation and manipulation of plastic: setting of detonator in plastic. The detonator must always be set on the opposite side and as far away as possible from the object to be demolished, as per sketch below:

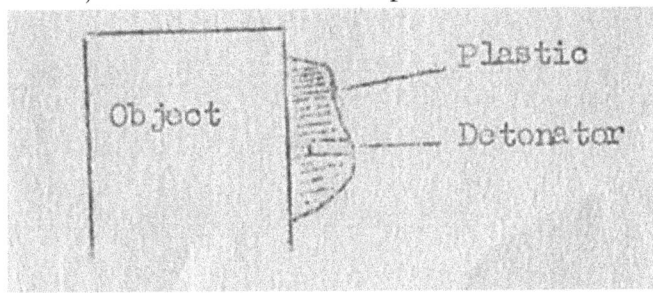

To render the blast of plastic more efficient pupils were taught to form a hollow inside the charge in the shape of a bell, as in the sketch below:

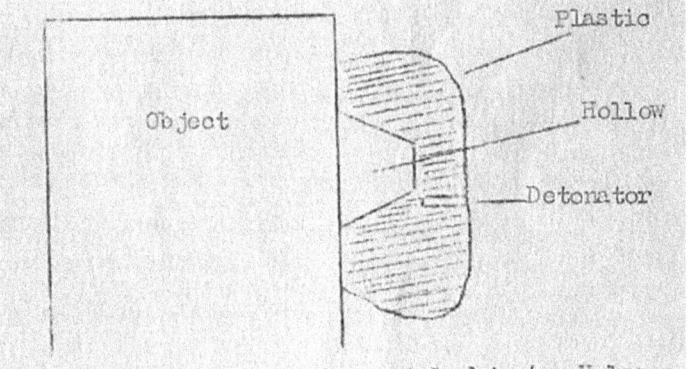

Plastic must never be cut with a metal object. Holes and hollows must be drilled with the finger of a piece of wood.

e) Preparation of liquid Tritol. Tritol can be liquified by heating the container in boiling water. It can then be placed in a bottle or any other small container, which makes it easy to conceal. Tritol, pupils were told, would not explode even if placed directly on a fire, it would merely burn. Tritol must never be cut with a metal object.

f) Preparation of plastic with magnets in cardboard boxes.

g) Practical course on time pencils dismantling and studying mechanism.

h) Practical course and examination of hand grenades and anti-personnel mines.

i) Preparation of small charges of industrial explosive.

40

j) Preparation and setting of charges on rails. (There was a piece of rail at the school).

k) Manipulation of incendiary box (1 Kg of esplosive powder). Drilling of hole in lid and introduction of detonator with time fuse, or time pencil.

l) Preparation of incendiary and explosive material connected together, (for petrol tanks).

m) Problems given by instructor. Measurements of piece of iron or wod, or gear wheel. Pupils had to calculate cross section and say how much explosive it required. In the case of a gear wheel and shaft the pupils had to find and indicate the most vulnerable point.

In a series of electric pylons pupils had to indicate the most important which should be destroyed.

4. Practical Exercises in the Garden of the Villa
   a) Ignition of celluloid incendiary box.
   b) Ignition of incendiary cylinder.
   c) Ignition of 1 Kg incendiary powder box.
   d) Examination of one British 15 cwt and one German Ford Truck. Pupils were told that the German Ford was identical to those built in the USA.

5. Practical Exercises in open ground behind the Villa
   a) Blowing up of rails with two charges of plastic. The experiment was not successful as the charges had been badly placed. The first charge cut the rail in half but the second was blown off without exploding.
   b) Application of 150 gr of plastic and incendiary cylinder of 500 gr on a half full petrol tank. Experiment not successful as the charge blew off the incendiary cylinder and the petrol did not catch fire.

c) Application of 150 gr of plastic with time fuse on top part of petrol camp. Experiment successful. The tank exploded and the petrol caught fire, (Experiment carried out by Subject).

6. Practical Exercises in Evacuated Villages

The pupils left the Villa in twos and met at a pre-arranged rendezvous. They were taken all together to an evacuated village where no one could see them and no one could hear the blast of the explosions.

The following experiments were carried out:

a) Firing three rounds with a Tommy gun on a piece of Tritol to prove that it would not explode.

b) Ignition of Tritol, Plastic and industrial explosive with time fuse. Pupils had to set the explosive on a stone and light the fuse, which was 20 cms long, and gave them 20 seconds to get away.

c) Ignition of three different charges by three pupils. This was to accustom pupils to danger. If one finished the job quicker than the others, the two others had to remain and finish their job while the first time fuse was burning.

d) Ignition of charge of explosive, hiding behind a tree during explosion, then coming out and firing three rounds with an 0.8 pistol on a target at 6 m distance. The target was 50 cms by 30 cms. (Five pupils out of twenty-four hit target).

e) Application of plastic, Tritol, and industrial explosives to blowing up of trees.

f) Application of four charges of plastic linked by detonating fuse.

g) Two methods of applying plastic to cylindrical objects such as trees, telegraph poles, etc.

i) Place charge in semi-circle round the tree or the pole.

ii) Divide the charge in two and place the two semi-circles facing each other, but with one approximately 3 cms above the other,. In this case the object is cut in two. The two charges can be connected with detonating fuse or with a detonator.

h) Demonstration of ineffectiveness of explosive if not attached on a target. A lump of plastic was hung on the branch of a tree and ignited. The plastic exploded, and the tree was undamaged.

i) Setting of a charge of plastic with a time pencil *half an hour).

j) Test of incendiary detonator on a charge of explosive. The charge did not explode.

VIII Range Practice

a) Seven rounds with 0.8 pencil on target at 25 m – standing. Time limit 30 seconds.

b) A pistol, an empty magazine, and seven rounds of ammunition were placed on a table. The pupil was given one minute to load the magazine and the pistol, and fire the seven rounds at 25 m distance.

c) Five rounds with 0.8 pistol at 50 m distance. No time limit.

d) Run 30 m. stop. Pick up pistol on the ground, remove safety catch, and fire five rounds at 50 m distance.

e) Fire fifteen rounds with a British Sten gun on target at 100 m distance. First five rounds: single shots; other ten rounds in bursts of two or three shots.

This took place once only, and not all pupils attended. (The best shots were Capt DI BELLA and FABBI. None of the others were any good at all).

IX Written questions after Visit to MILAN Central Station

What advantages does trail transport offer for sabotage as opposed to MT [Military Trucks] transport?

Which are the most vulnerable points in rail transport?

a) Fixed installations
b) Rolling stock
c) Goods (on trucks or in warehouses)

Possibilities of sabotage with explosives or incendiaries
Describe the most vulnerable point to attack. Charges and
quantity of explosive which should be used. Sketches of
fuses. Remarks on damage which might be caused.
Possibilities of sabotage without explosives or incendiaries
Describe vulnerable objectives. Describe how the sabotage
is to be carried out. Remarks on damage which might be
done.
Suggestions on new methods or new objectives
Similar questions were asked after the two lorries had been
examined by the pupils (See VI.4.d)

X Recommendations made to pupils on their behaviour
before, during and after an act of sabotage.
Pupils were advised never to leave traces behind in any place.
They must avoid going to hotels, but always ask for shelter
with peasants or, if in towns and villages, with private families,
where they did not need to register.
They must not make themselves conspicuous in any way and
especially not spend too much money. If they were sent to
Allied Occupied Territory they should pass themselves off as
refugees who had come over to escape forced labour in
GERMANY, and try and find themselves a job. Those who
had families in the South should say they had come across to
join their relatives.

Approach to Objective
Pupils were told that many objectives in Allied Occupied
Territory, such as petrol and ammunition dumps, were not
properly guarded or not guarded at all; the sentries were few
and too careless.
For the sabotage of trucks the best method was to wait at a
café or restaurant where a driver might stop for a drink and
seize the opportunity when he left the truck unguarded.

Alternatively a saboteur could ask for a lift and leave a charge in the vehicle just before leaving it.

For railway sabotage pupils were advised to look for jobs as waggon workers so as to obtain a pass to enable them to enter a station, and also to circulate freely during curfew hours.

In general pupils did not have any specific target assigned to them and it was left to their initiative to find suitable objectives. Some, like Subject himself, did not know of any targets in Allied Occupied Territory, but others, who were natives of TUSCANY, had already pre-arranged targets such as power lines, aquaducts, railways, etc, no details available.) (Comment: Subject in any case had been told he would be used as a post-occupational agent).

To throw a piece of explosive charcoal in a railway tender pupils were instructed to pretend to be normal passengers and to be throwing back a piece of coal that had fallen out of the tender. (They practiced at MILAN Central Station).

After the Act of Sabotage
Pupils were advised to return to the spot and mix with the crowd that would collect to see the damage so as to have a change to have a good look and report on their return a success or failure.

They were told never to run away after having committed an act of sabotage so as not to attract attention., but leave the place very quietly. The time fuse should always be sufficiently long or the time pencil set in such a way that they would give the saboteur ample time to get away safely and without having to hurry.

After they had been paired off pupils were told that if they met another saboteur known to them they must ignore him completely and not speak to him under any pretext. They were never to tell other couples where they were going or even where they had been or what acts of sabotage they had carried out or attempted to carry out.

They were told they were sent in couples so that one man could bolster the other's morale when necessary, and also to watch each other and avoid betrayal; also to avoid one man boasting of having carried out acts of sabotage which he had not really done. Finally so that one man could watch while the other was setting the charge.

If a saboteur was called up for military service while in Allied Occupied Territory he should answer the call so as to avoid trouble with the Italian authorities and AMG [Allied Military Government], but he was then to carry out sabotage in the Army.

Pupils were told that they would be watched by German agents in Allied Occupied Territory. (Ibid.)

April 1945

In April 1945, Mario Rossi was arrested in Milan and, during interrogation, admitted that he was the leader of an X MAS stay-behind organisation with agents in Turin, Genoa, Bologna, Milan and Venice. Whether he handed himself in to the Allies or was arrested following denunciation was not reported. Information he provided led to other arrests, agents being interned, and over the following months, the X MAS organisation was dismantled.

VEGA Bn., X Flotilla MAS had a section in GENOA under the command of Mario ROSSI.

ROSSI was found to be already under arrest as a political suspect. His arrest had been carried out by the C.L.N. [Committee for National Liberation] BOGLIASCO at the end of April 1945.

On the 21st May 1945 he was transferred to the F.S.S. Section of the MARASSI Prison.

Interrogated briefly by an officer of S.C.I. on 22nd May 1945 he gave the following information.

A. Personal Particulars:

Name: Mario ROSSI
Born: 24/12/1910 at PIEVE LIGURE (GENOA)
Address: Via Aurelia 20, PIEVE LIGURE

B. Circumstances Leading to Organisation of Post-Occupational Group.

In December 1944, ROSSI, then serving with the X Flotilla MAS, was requested to take command of a new battalion composed of the picked men of X Flotilla MAS.

BORGHESE suggested that the number required would be about 50; all persons who were not known as prominent Fascists but who were loyal Italians.

ROSSI set about choosing the personal [sic] at once. In March 1945, BORGHESE again called for him and inspected the progress made. He then instructed ROSSI to divide them into teams to cover the following cities: - MILAN, GENOA, TURIN, BOLOGNA and VENICE.

SEGRETO

lì, 2 Giugno 1945

Nella presente relazione sono contenute le fotografie ed i nominativi di ufficiali paracadutisti repubblicani.

I dati sono stati forniti da ufficiale e sottufficiale di questo Gruppo.-

- CUCCHIARA Elio - Tenente di Fregata istruttore paracadutisti Repubblicani (Relazione 193/Zi).

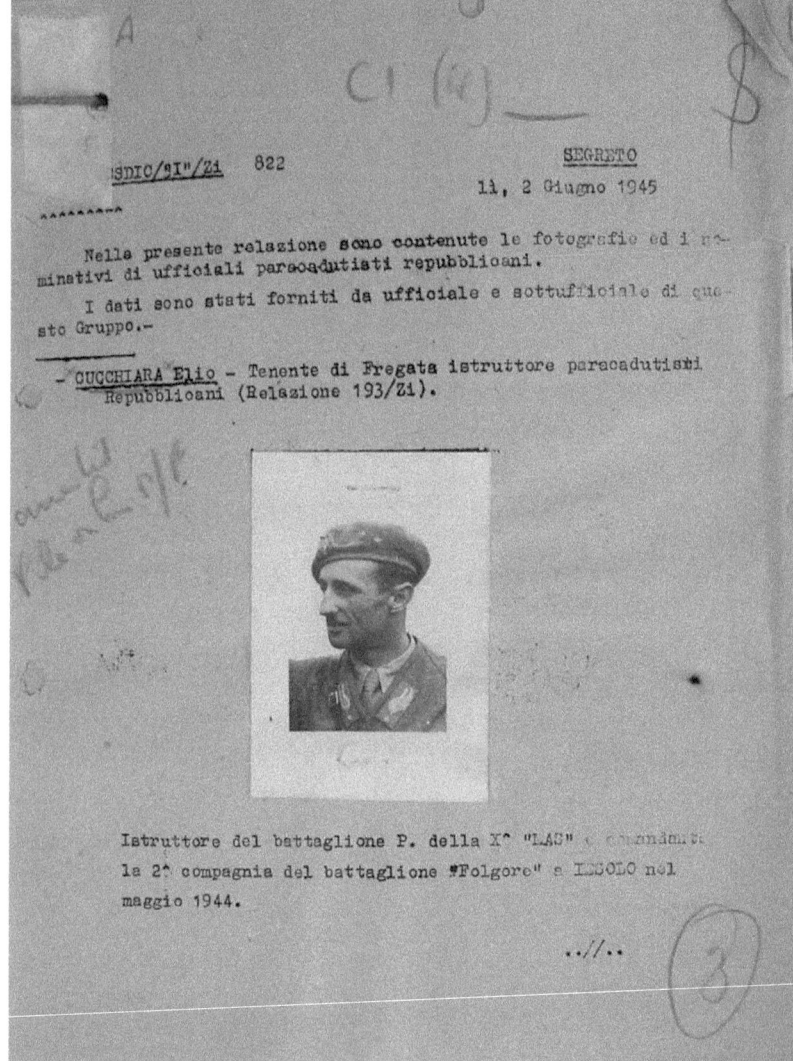

Istruttore del battaglione P. della X° "LAS" e comandante la 2ª compagnia del battaglione "Folgore" a ISSOLO nel maggio 1944.

..//..

(TNA WO204/12453

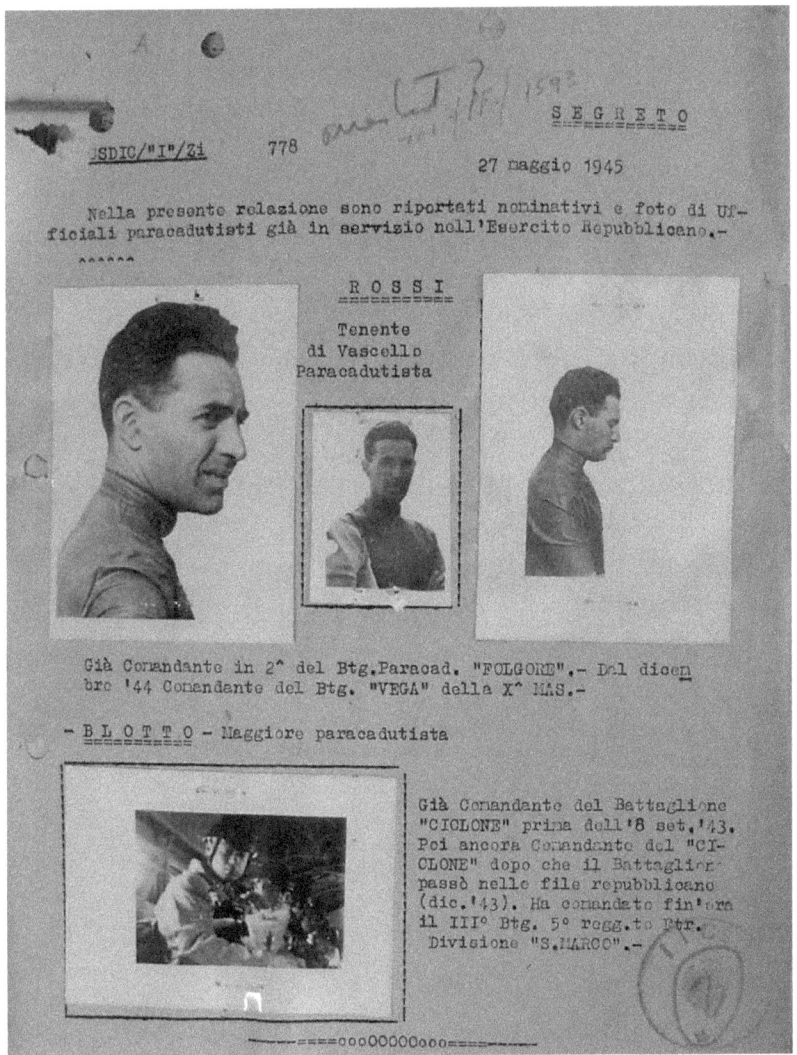

(TNA WO204/12453)
SECRET
Preliminary Interrogation Report on Mario ROSSI
C.   Circumstances Leading to Arrest:

S.C.I. Genoa was informed by S.C.I. Milan that a post-
occupational organisation composed of members of the Final
Orders:
The final orders of BORGHESE were as follows: -

i)   All members would wear civilian clothes and remain hidden in
the city in which they were to operate.

ii)   They were all to be paid six month's pay in advance.
iii)   Each city was to have W/T station.
iv)   The main funds for each city were to be invested in a
        transport organisation which would carry on a legitimate
        business, in cooperation with the local authorities and the
        Committee of Liberation. (Thereby increasing the capital and
        at the same time having transport available for the purposes
        of the organisation.)
v)   No activities of any kind were to be undertaken until concise
        orders were received from BORGHESE.

    D. Organisation:

The group at GENOA was organised as follows: -

i)   O.C. Mario ROSSI
ii)   Financial Cover – Carlo FRASSONI, Manager of the
        Transport Company/
        Assisted by: Dionino FRASSONI
                       Alessandro FRASSONI
                       Alberico ANGELI
iii) Information Group – (furnished with W/T station)
O.C. Lieut. Giovanni LINETTI
W/T Operator   CAMI
Lieut. Aldo   BERTUCCI
2/Lt. Sergio   PIA
                 RIGHETTO
Alessandro   BERGAMO
                 VATTERONI
Burgatta   CONSALVO
                 LACAGNINA
                 BORGONOVO
                 DOGA
                 STAGNI
Renzo   BARTOLI
iv) Sabotage Group (Furnished with explosives and arms.)
O.C. Lieut. MANTINI alias Eng. Mario BIANCHINI
                 CINI Ulisse
                 RAMASSO
                 NAPOLITANO Euginio

	NAPOLITANO (Brother of last named)
Sgt.	LEGOVINI Marcello
	TREVISAN Aldo
S/Capo	ERCOLINO Antonio
	MIELESI Vilfrido
	ZANELLA Saverio
	ALBERI Italo
	CAZZANIGA Emilio
	ARDITO Stefano
	OSSI Giuseppe.

NOTE: (a) Lt. MANTINI was originally sent to E.O.T. [Enemy Occupied Territory] on a mission on behalf of Fifth Army. He however abandoned this and joined the X Flotilla MAS. ROSSI now understands that he has gone to FLORENCE to contact the Allied officer whom he previously knew.

(b) The W/T set was consigned by the operator, CAMI, to the Italian Naval Command, GENOA. ROSSI does not know if he later withdrew it or not.

(c) Should there be any danger in the port of GENOA, the sabotage group were to assist the local Committee of Liberation in saving it thereby forming a useful cover for themselves with the local partisans and also saving the port for ITALY.

(d) ROSSI cannot remember the exact distribution of the group's funds as all that side was handled by the group's accountant, Lieut. Giuseppe GOZZI, at present in MILAN.

(e) At least a large part of the explosives were hidden near SORI (an area of GENOA). ROSSI understands that they were found and seized by the Partisans.

F. Comments:

i) It appears that the exact functions of the group were not yet determined. BORGHESE wished to have a nucleus at his command to further his own ambitions at a later date (possibly after the termination of the Allied occupation). It is possible it would not have been used against the Allies against the Communists.

ii) The group formed a threat to Allied security and it would certainly have obeyed any orders given by BORGHESE, without reference to the Allied authorities.

Supplementary interrogation report on Mario ROSSI

ROSSI has furnished the following additional information:

1. Antonio PRETO (Arrested) In Sept/Oct 1944 Prince
    BORGHESE ordered ROSSI to put a party of 10-12
    saboteurs at the Disposal of the Germans. A party of
    volunteers was assembled under the command of Antonio
    PRETO.

    This group reported to the Germans at VERONA where they
    learned they were to cross the lines in civilian clothes. Half of
    the group thereupon refused to attempt the task and returned
    to the X Flotilla MAS.

    PRETO band at the head of the remainder. They remained in
    VERONA until December 1944 when PRETO told ROSSI
    that they were about to cross the lines in the LUCCA area.

    In February 1945 one of the party returned and told ROSSI
    that the mission had not succeeded as there was at that time
    an offensive and the party had had to return through the lines.
    Shortly afterwards all the party except PRETO and one sailor
    returned to the X Flotilla MAS.

    On about 8 – 9 April 1945 PRETO himself returned and said
    he had been released from the service of the Germans. He
    asked to join the VEGA Bn.

2. Teodore SCHULTZ. In March 1945 ROSSI met a certain
    Teodore SCHULTZ, a Swiss citizen, who had a mission on
    behalf of the Germans, to cross the lines with a small bag of
    diamonds which he was to deliver in the Vatican.

    SCHULTZ attempted to cross in the LUCCA area in the
    company of two members of the X Flotilla MAS, namely
    CHECK and ROSSI. The attempt failed and all three
    returned.

    The description of SCHULTZ is as follows: -
    Age 30 years; height 1.68m; blondish chestnut hair; small
    moustache; but teeth; thin build; has Swiss passport – in
    order. [Copies of these details would have been published on
    a wanted list disseminated to all checkpoints.]

3. Comments:

ROSSI has everything to assist the 85 FSS to track other members of the organisation. He appears to be sincere and stating that he never intended it to operate against the allies. He is a good type and has certainly valuable information regarding the activities of Prince BORGHESE, the X FLOTILLA MAS, the VEGA Bn. post-occupational organisation etc.

4.   Recommendation:

It is recommended that ROSSI be further interrogated by CSDIC, FLORENCE, chiefly to assist and checking on the statements of Prince BORGHESE.

The assistance given by him to the Allied authorities should be borne in mind when his ultimate disposal is decided upon. JGF 31 May 1945 (Ibid.)

May 1945

Lt. Col. Stephen Springarn, Chief of the US 5th Army Counter
Intelligence Corps in Italy (Lori Stewart
https://www.dvidshub.net/image/8128570/tactical-ci-italy-nov-
1944)

American Lt. Colonel Stephen Springarn was Chief of the 5th
Army's Counter Intelligence Corps in Italy. In that capacity, he was
sent copies of all interrogation reports of captured enemy agents
giving him an overview of the German Intelligence Service and the
operations of their Italian collaborators. In a post-war interview he
admitted,

> I was a counterespionage officer during the war and I was
> commanding officer of the 5th Army Counter Intelligence

54

Corps for two years, from the end of the African and throughout the Italian campaign. I was in the Salerno invasion, I was at Anzio and at Cassino and at many other places, and while I was not a combat officer I saw a lot of people get killed, close by. We went into new cities with the assault troops and did the initial counterintelligence work, grabbing the human targets of whom we had advance information, and trying to grab the documents too, at the intelligence centers and places like that, and other things. And we captured, the counterintelligence personnel at 5th Army in the Italian Campaign, captured approximately 525 German spies and saboteurs. They were mostly Italians, but they were working for the German intelligence services, Abwehr and SD (Sicherheitsdienst – the Intelligence Service of the SS and the Nazi Party. The Schutzstaffel was a paramilitary security organisation], which I believe is more than any other Allied army captured during World War II. I don't have any figures on the Russians, but as far as I know it was better than any of the Western allies, and we often modestly stated that it was more than the FBI had caught in the whole forty years of its history. (Spingarn, Stephen J.; Hess, Jerry N. (20 March 1967). "Oral History Interview with Stephen J. Spingarn (1)". Harry S. Truman Library & Museum.)

The CIC played a vital role in apprehending and interrogating members of the X MAS stay-behind organisations. In the 'Counter Intelligence Corps History and Mission in World War II,' it stated that CIC

…immediately took over control of the city pending the arrival of either a control group from Division or from AMGOT [Allied Military Government of Occupied Territories]. Immediate steps were taken to control the municipality, the Carabinieri, the police and prisons, business activities, public utilities, and military and political organizations and their headquarters. The Church was asked to cooperate: and after necessary conferences with the leading military, civil, and religious authorities, a proclamation was issued imposing the necessary restrictions on the civil and political life of the community. Everything was done to assist the local representative of the Division Commander, and later of AMGOT, in bringing the community back to normal without interfering or delaying the accomplishment of the combat mission of the Division. The work of the section was completed when it turned over its responsibilities to either the Corps Counter Intelligence Corps section, or the representative of AMGOT. [...]

The major effort of the Counter Intelligence Corps was made in captured towns. Counter Intelligence Corps personnel restored order; secured documents, critical installations, and supplies: arrested leading Fascists; and investigated the civil administrators. AWGOT officers were kept informed of the political situation, and replacements were recommended for officials arrested. During the interim between capture by combat troops and the taking over of the communities by AMOT personnel, many civil problems related to security were met. [...]

In December, 1943, an event occurred to ease the personnel situation. An Italian counterespionage organization SIBI CS (Sicurezza Informazione Militare, Contro-Spionaggio) was attached to the Fifth Army and placed under the operational direction of the Fifth Army Counter Intelligence Corps. This unit proved itself invaluable in the conduct of undercover counterintelligence missions which would have been practically impossible for the Counter Intelligence Corps to accomplish. This unit averaged about 50 men, of whom 30 operated with Army Counter Intelligence Corps. The others were deployed with the Corps and Division Counter Intelligence Corps detachments.

A major development in the operations of the Counter Intelligence Corps was the establishment in December of the Fifth, Army Refugee Interrogation Post. The principal task of this new organization was the interrogation of civilian suspects who had not been identified as enemy agents by the arresting units. Some 40 enemy agents were detected by the Refugee Interrogation Post which, through continuous interrogation, had acquired exceptional knowledge of the many German Intelligence Service organizations in Italy, their personalities, and set-ups. The work of the Fifth Army Refugee Interrogation

Post received many commendations from Allied intelligence authorities in this theater. [...]

In the early part of April, 1944, Army Counter Intelligence Corps moved from Caserta to Sparanise where the Counter Intelligence Corps sub-sections were also deployed around the Army area to provide area coverage. Here a system of civilian control was introduced which later culminated in successful counterintelligence activities. Carabinieri road blocks were established throughout the area. Coast-watching posts were established to supervise all landings. Counter Intelligence Corps screening units also were set up at the AMG Refugee Camps. Persons registering at hotels or boarding houses in towns throughout the area were subject to investigation, as were persons obtaining new identity cards or ration cards. Spot checks were made of strangers, and roving patrols of counter-sabotage or Counter Intelligence Corps personnel supplemented the stationary Carabinieri check-posts along the highways. This control system grew as Counter Intelligence Corps experience gradually increased.

On 24 May, 1944, most of the Fifth Army Counter Intelligence Corps Detachment joined the Rome "S" Force at a concentration area near Naples, leaving behind only a skeleton force to cover the Army area during their absence. The purpose of the 'S" Force was to enter the city with the first troops and provide immediate intelligence and counterintelligence action against personality and building targets. The security personnel consisted of about 100, of whom 50 were American Counter Intelligence Corps personnel (from Fifth Army Counter Intelligence Corps, Counter Intelligence Corps Peninsular Base Section, and Counter Intelligence Corps Combat Advance Section, and the Counter Intelligence Corps Detachment newly organized to handle Rome after its capture), and the remaining 50 were British Field Security personnel. All of the security personnel were placed under Fifth Army Counter Intelligence Corps direction.

The "S" Force moved to Anzio by boat at the end of May and entered Rome on schedule on the night of 4-5 June. During the first 15 days in Rome, its Counter Intelligence Corps and FSS personnel seized a vast amount of important intelligence and counterintelligence documents and apprehended a considerable number of known enemy agents. Counter Intelligence Corps personnel with this Force received written commendation from the "SW Force commander for their work. On 17 June, the Counter Intelligence Corps, Fifth Army, left "S" Force, moving to Tuscania where it resumed its normal functions. [...]

From October, 1944, to April, 1945, a total of 200 trained enemy agents were captured in Fifth Army areas, an average of over one a day. The Counter Intelligence Corps represented less than half of the operational counterintelligence personnel in that area. The excellent control systems of the 92nd Division and IV Corps Counter Intelligence Corps made the capture of a great many of these agents possible, and those that filtered through were frequently caught by the Army Counter Intelligence Corps. In addition, the Army Counter Intelligence Corps was able to ferret out a number of post-occupation espionage agents, some of whom had built up good cover stories. Interrogation of enemy agents captured by the 305th Counter Intelligence Corps Detachment made possible the capture of a considerable number of other agents outside the 305th's area by other counterintelligence agencies.

THE GERMAN ESPIONAGE PROBLEM. The drive from Rome to the Arno River was too rapid to permit effective counterintelligence. It was possible only to skim the surface in order to move along with the troops. Because of the few captures of enemy agents, there was actually a dearth of information about the German Intelligence Service (GIS) in Italy. Little was learned concerning its methods and techniques, and without this information it was extremely difficult to capture German agents. However, the enemy also was hungry for some intelligence concerning Allied plans and operations, since it was evident to him that the Allied advance would steam roller through the Italian peninsula. To obtain this information he decided to dispatch trained agents behind the Allied lines.

Beginning October, 1944, a mass assault of German espionage and sabotage agents on the Fifth Army area began. Some were parachuted in, some landed by boat on the coast, but the majority were linecrossers, most of whom entered the Fifth Army area in the thinly held Western sector. b.

Fortunately, by this time the Counter Intelligence Corps had tightened its system of controls and was constantly improving the system. Dr. Kora, the German officer in charge of Abwehr Kommando 190, which ran large numbers of espionage agents into the Fifth Army area confessed after capture that not a single one of his agents had returned between October, 1944, and January, 1945. Similar admissions were made by other captured German officials.

From October, 1944, to April, 1945 a total of 200 trained enemy agents were captured in Fifth Army areas, an average of over one a day. The Counter Intelligence Corps represented less than half of the operational counterintelligence personnel in that area. The excellent control systems of the 92nd Division and IV Corps Counter Intelligence Corps made the capture of a great many of these agents possible, and those that filtered through were frequently caught by the Army Counter Intelligence Corps. In addition, the Army Counter Intelligence Corps was able to ferret out a number of post-occupation espionage agents, some of whom had built up good cover stories. Interrogation of enemy agents captured by the 305th Counter Intelligence Corps Detachment made possible the capture of a considerable number of other agents outside the 305th's area by other counterintelligence agencies.

After the initial assault the German Intelligence Service was forced to rely on emergency measures to recruit new agents to replace those who had not returned. In Northern Italy the Abwehr opened several spy schools, recruiting poor peasants, black-market operators, Fascists, and former officers of the Italian Air Force and Navy. Their recruits ranged from twelve-year old boys to middle-aged men and women. There was even a half-wit, an innocent soul who agreed to cross the lines for two dollars in Italian lire. These recruits were given a short three-week course in espionage and sabotage and then dispatched to the front lines to do their work. They sought quantity rather than quality. The German pattern became so methodical and exact that the American Counter Intelligence Corps stood in wait for these agents to cross the lines.

American Counter Intelligence Corps agents, through their personal interrogation of captured enemy agents, had become familiar with the complicated German Intelligence Service's

Italian set-up and with those characteristics which distinguished its agents.

To insure counterintelligence coverage, the 85th Division provided for a Counter Intelligence Corps team to accompany each regimental combat team. Since the troops of this Division were occupying areas already covered by sub-sections of the IV Corps and Fifth Army Counter Intelligence Corps, its Counter Intelligence Corps detachment established liaison with those Counter Intelligence Corps units already in the area. Emphasis was placed on the importance of apprehending all suspicious or unidentifiable persons for questioning by the Counter Intelligence Corps. Due to the continual advance into enemy territory, and because of the frequent replacements of personnel in Divisions, it was necessary to provide the combat troops with constant training in security and to reemphasize the basic rules of security and how they were related to the mission of the Counter Intelligence Corps.

In late December the Fifth Army Counter Intelligence Corps Headquarters moved from Tavernelle to Campi Bisenzio effecting little change in the area of coverage since the various detachments were providing coverage for one another in most areas.

THE FINAL BREATHROUGH. By mid-April the Fifth Army Counter Intelligence Corps was ready to perform its usual "S" Force mission in the major cities along the line of advance. On the 21st Bologna fell, and the Fifth Army Counter Intelligence Corps entered the city as the "S" Force. During the first four days of intensive activity, numerous persons of security interest, as well as German Intelligence Service officials, were apprehended. After five days in which the Counter Intelligence Corps had been engaged in handling these captured enemy agents and officials, as well as effecting the capture of valuable intelligence documents, the Fifth Army Counter Intelligence Corps moved to Verona, the headquarters of the German Intelligence Service in Italy. Thereafter the Germans retreated rapidly out of Italy, and on 2 May, the war in Italy came to an end. This, however, did not terminate the activities of the Counter Intelligence Corps which continued to seek out the German Intelligence Service officials who had gone into hiding. (https://irp.fas.org/agency/army/cic-wwii.pdf)

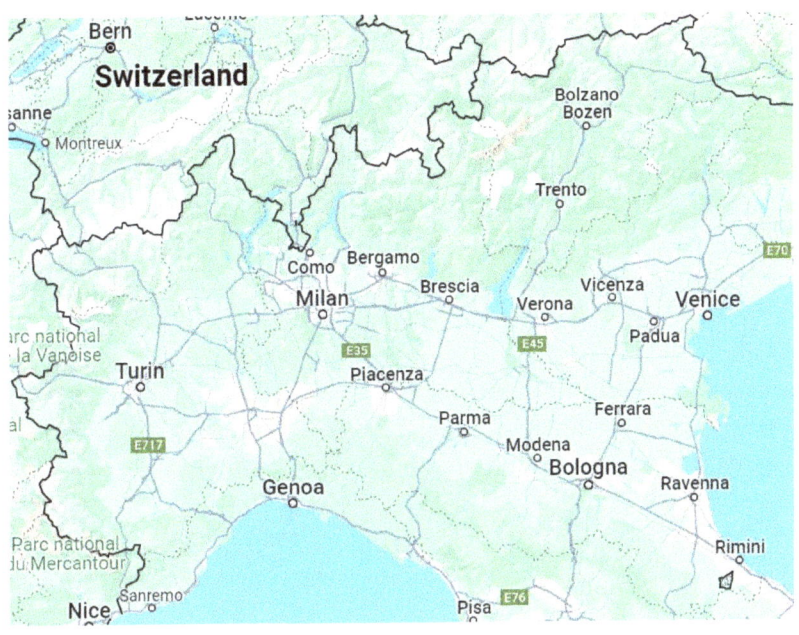

On 9 April 1945, British, Polish, Indian and New Zealand troops, accompanied by Italian partisans and combat forces under the command of General Mark Clark, launched an attack against German troops holding a defensive line southwest of Bologna. By 21 April, the city was liberated. An insurrection in Genoa on 23 April succeeded in driving the Germans out of the city and the Allies arrived on 27 April. On 25 April the National Liberation Committee of Upper Italy made up of liberals, socialists, communists and others, called for a general insurrection against Nazi-fascists in all occupied territories. Partisans liberated Turin and Milan on the same day. An insurrection in Venice on 27 April ended with the German surrender on 29 April. General Heinrich von Vietinghoff, on behalf of the German and RSI forces in Italy signed the document at the Royal Palace of Caserta. Approximately one million Germans surrendered in Italy and Austria,

The CIC began a search for German-trained stay-behind agents in the major towns and cities. Their experiences since arriving in Southern Italy in 1943, had shown them that the Abwehr had trained Italian Fascists for stay-behind espionage and sabotage operations against the Allies. (TNA WO 204/11692; WO204/12369; WO/204/12397; WO/204/12398)

The capture and interrogation of X MAS personnel during their operations against Allied shipping between 1940 and 1943 had allowed Britain's Counter Intelligence Service and Counter-Sabotage section to build up a comprehensive knowledge of the Italian organisation, its personnel, its training schools, their syllabus and their equipment.

With Italy's Armistice, officers from Britian's Royal Navy and the American Navy liaised with Ernesto Forza, the Commander of X MAS surface section who had been based in Taranto, Southern Italy. His loyal supporters who had been interned were released to form a new naval assault unit, the Mariassalto.. (https://comocompanion.com/2020/04/27/comos-lake-montor fano-commandos-contraband-and-the-cia/comment-page-1/#respond)

Using details from Paul Kemp's *Underwater Warriors*, the Wikipedia entry for the X MAS Flotilla reported that,

The *Mariassalto* was set up at Taranto alongside the British frogman force in the Mediterranean. Forza was pleased to demonstrate Italian expertise in this area to the British, and the group was also keen to be in action, though if they were caught they would almost certainly have been shot.

In June 1944 came an opportunity to take action, in Operation QWZ, a joint mission against targets in La Spezia harbour. The attack was against the Italian cruisers *Bolzano* and *Gorizia*, which had been taken by the Germans after the Italian surrender. This was to thwart a German plan to sink them where they would block the harbour entrance. The mission also aimed to attack German U-boats in the harbour. British chariots would attack the cruisers whilst Mariassalto's Gamma Frogmen would attack U-boats penned in the harbour. On 2 June 1944 the Italian destroyer *Grecale* sailed from Bastia in Corsica to La Spezia carrying three speedboats, and Italian frogmen including Luigi Durand De La Penne, and two British chariots. [The 'Chariot' was a British-designed manned torpedo based on the SLC.]

One chariot broke down and was abandoned, though the other successfully sank *Bolzano*. However, the *Gamma* men were unsuccessful in their attack on the U-boat pens. All the participants escaped, linking with partisan groups on land.

In April 1945 a final mission, Operation Toast, was planned. This was aimed at sinking the newly converted shipping liner now the aircraft carrier *Aquila*, just completed in Genoa. For this *Mariassalto* men would make use of two British chariots, as they had none of their own SLCs available. On 18 April 1945 the destroyer *Legionario*, carrying two high-speed motorboats equipped with chariots sailed from Venice for Genoa led by Captain Chavasse SOE and Forza. Both chariots were deployed and succeeded in penetrating the defences but found the hull of *Aquila* so encrusted with barnacles and seaweed the limpet mines could not be attached to it. The frogmen had to lay the charges on the seafloor of the outer harbour mole and when the charge exploded as planned the ship remained afloat in spite of the attack. All of the frogmen escaped safely. The German commander never put his extensive demolition plans for Genoa into action and thus Aquila was never sunk as a blockade to the harbour. (Kemp, Paul, *Underwater Warriors*, Arms and Armour Press, 1997, pp.61-64; https://en.wikipedia.org/wiki/Decima_Flottiglia_MAS)

The comandosupremo website reported that Luigi Durand de la Penn, one of the X MAS raiders who attacked the British Fleet in Alexandria, trained agents of the American Office of Strategic Services (OSS). This naval special force later became known as US Navy Seals. (http://www.comandosupremo.com/strike-on-alexandria.html)

The use of X MAS personnel by the British and American navies was documented in another War Office file in the National Archives, entitled: 'Liquidation of X Decima MAS'. At the end of the war, personnel attached to military and intelligence units were either returned to 'civvy street', the euphemism for a civilian existence, or, if their services were still considered useful, employed by MI5 or MI6.

The first document in the 'Liquidation' file was a letter from Captain D. Gurvey, acting for the Acting Chief of Staff, (G-2) to his counterparts in the Fifth Army and Allied Forces HQ. Dated 28 May 1945, it stated:

Ref. Your CI-249 dated 24 May, forwarding Roster XIII from PIACENZA PW Stockade.
All these officers of X Flotilla MAS, viz: =
Capt. FARIANA Luigi
S.Ten GRITA, Carmela
Ten OLIVIERI Vittorio
Ten. Col. PATRIZI Constantino
S. Ten STADONI Sauro
should be separated and forwarded to the CI Compound at ANCONA. (TNA WO204/12452)

Borghese's interrogation May 1945

In the spring of 1945, realising that Germany was not going to win the war with the Allies, General Karl Wolff, Chief of Police and SS Commander in Italy, met Allen Dulles, the head of the American Office of Strategic Services (OSS) in Switzerland. OSS was the United States Intelligence Service during the Second World War. Wolff wanted to negotiate a separate truce for his men in Italy. Fearing that Borghese would face the same fate as Mussolini for the crimes of the X MAS against the partisans, he requested that the Americans ensures that he should receive 'honourable treatment'.

Dulles was true to his word. With the assistance of Captain Angleton, the Head of the SCI/Z Units, Borghese was dressed in American uniform and driven by two Americans from Milan to Rome on 25 April. Provided with food and accommodation, he was then interrogated. (https://biographics.org/junio-valerio-borghese-the-black-prince-of-world-war-ii/; Sergio Nesi, Italian Supreme Court report in *Il processo*, in *Junio Valerio Borghese. Un principe, un comandante, un italiano*. Bologna, Lo Scarabeo, 2004, pp. 555-556; Kisatsky, Deborah, *The United States and the European Right, 1945-1955*. Ohio State University Press, 2005)

His interrogation report, a copy of which is in the National Archives in Kew, covers thirty typed pages relating to the pre- and post-armistice X MAS activities. Some were more detailed than others. One has to imagine that specialist British interrogators would have elicited a longer report, given the attacks made by him and his men against British targets. He claimed that he was concerned that after the armistice, the Germans had used some X MAS personnel for sabotage activities over which he had no control.

He officially announced to HARSTER [Head of German Security and SD] that in future the X Flotilla MAS would carry out sabotage work of its own and would require all its available personnel for the purpose. Partly in order to lend some plausibility to this declaration, a reorganisation of the NP Bn was put into effect, its B Ech, [?echelon], expanded by men combed out from the combatant ranks, being formed into a new battalion known as the VEGA Bn, which was henceforth to provide the personnel for special undertakings. BORGHESE at the same time planned to create a post-occupational sabotage and espionage network in the five principal North Italian cities, and instructed ROSSI to prepare the necessary plans. At the same time he requested HARSTER to give his consent to the creation of these groups as it was foreseen that without the knowledge and cooperation of the SD they might have had difficulty in establishing themselves and would even be liable to arrest. HARSTER apparently agreed in principle but a written laisser-passer from his office was never received. [...] (TNA WO204/12803. The report refers to a CSDIC note on the Vega Bn and the history of the post-occupational network (CSDIC/CMF/SD 73 para 2) but, as yet, it has not come to light.)

Formation of VEGA Battalion:
Following his talk with HARSTER sometime during October, Subject established the so-called VEGA Battalion under the command of Tenente di Vascello ROSSI. The purpose behing the formation of the new battalion was to place all personnel hereto=fore concerned with espionage or sabotage under the direction of a dingle unit. In line with this purpose, the NP Units which up to this time had been in the German Service, were transferred to the VEGA Battalion. BUTAZZONU himself was removed from all contact with sabotage or espionage activities and his men converted to straight infantry use. The work of the VEGA Battalion was conceived as:
a. Gathering intelligence information in AOT.
b. The commission of acts of sabotage in AOT.
c. The preparation of post-occupation espionage and sabotage in the main Northern Italian centers.
ROSSI was in complete charge of this activity and kept Subject informed through regular reports of the progress along the three lines indicated.

Preparation of 10th MAS Pin Groups:
With regard to the preparation of post-occupation groups in Northern Italian cities, Subject states that the activity of the VEGA Battalion proceeded simultaneously with similar activity carried out by the GIS, by the Republican Fascist Intelligence Service under PAVOLINI and probably by the MGIR [?]. All of these, according to Subject, were working separately. During November and December, ROSSI presented a program for the establishment of five 10th MAS groups of post-occupational agents, namely in MILAN, TURIN, GENOA, BOLOGNA and VENICE. The Venice group was to have its headquarters in the city but to work throughout the whole Veneto area. Each group was to be composed of six or more men and, in all, according to Subject, the number of VEGA Battalion personnel who volunteered for the work was between 60 and 70. Each group was to be provided with a portable W/T set, arms and explosives. In each city various forms of commercial cover were to be used. The objectives of the group, according to Subject, were strictly military operations. ROSSI, he states, was the only one who knew all the details of the plan. During the course of the winter he came to MILAN every week or two to explain the progress achieved, to get additional funds, etc. The details ROSSI presented in the form of regular reports which, according to Subject, are in the archives of the 10th MAS at his Headquarters in the Castello di Lonato at LONATO. Others who knew to a greater or lesser extent of the program were UXA and 2nd Lt. Ottavio MORBELLI. The latter was head of the Subject's secretariat and therefore received all of the reports and was responsible for their safekeeping and filing.

Placing and Last News of the Pin Groups:
The components of the respective post-occupational groups were placed during February and March [1945]. According to the plan, the groups were to keep in W/T communication with Subject, whose base was to be located first at Milan and then at some undetermined point either in the mountains or the German "Reduit". Subject stresses that the entire program was based on the assumption that the Allied occupation of Northern Italy would be gradual, and therefore that there would be ample opportunity to provide for the withdrawal to

other headquarters as the Allied armies approached. Subject states that as far as he knows, the groups received no orders with regards to the eventuality of an armistice. He considers that this was a fundamental error on his part but believes that none of the group would work following the cessation of military hostilities. Subject saw ROSSI for the last time at the end of March or the 1st of April, but only for a brief moment.

Castello di Lonato, X MAS HQ in 1944-5
(https://www.xtremeadventure.it/castello-di-lonato/)

Borghese's HQ in Castello di Lonato
(https://www.grandigiardini.it/lang_EN/170-visit-Rocca-di-Lonato-del-Garda-event-tickets)

He was told that LOCASIO (identical with the LOCASCIO mentioned in the interrogation of LOCATELLI had been captured by partisans. Following this, Subject had no further reports, he did not see ROSSI again, and therefore does not know what decisions were taken with regard to the operations of the groups, but again states with certainty that, as the purposes were strictly military and devoid of any post-defeat aspects, none of the groups would continue operations.

Pin Group Personalities Concerned:
Inasmuch as ROSSI was in complete charge of all activities of the VEGA Battalion in general and of the pin group in particular, Subject states that he himself recalls only a few of the people concerned in the post-occupational program. He has heard the name of Rino GRASSO. UXA, Subject states, as Commandant of the 10th MAS, as au courant of all operational activities; the VEGA Battalion as a component of his command therefore came under his observation. According to Subject, however, UXA was completely out of the planning and execution of the post-occupational groups.

Signora Fede Arnaud POCEK, head of the 10th MAS Women's Auxiliary, Subject states, had absolutely nothing to do with the post-occupational program.

Lieut. Giuseppe GOZZI, in his capacity as 10th MAS paymaster, would probably know more of the details, next to ROSSIm, than any other person concerned. Subject recalls that large sums of money were given GOZZI for the use of the groups and both GOZZI and ROSSI were made personally responsible by Subject for the expenditure of all funds. Subject recalls that Lieut. Giovanni DEL CAMPERIO was one of the members of the post-occupational team. He recalls that Lieut. Elio CUCCHIARI, an expert saboteur with several missions to AOT to his credit, was another pin group member.

Aside from these, however, Subject states that none of the other VEGA members concerned are recalled by him, nor does he recall any details of the commercial cover established in each city. He states that following the placing of the post-occupational groups those who remained of the VEGA Battalion numbering about 140, were re-assigned to other units and the VEGA Battalion itself was dissolved in March 1945.

Interrogator's Comments:
Subject has given every indication of complete willingness to co-operate, and great care and insistence has been placed during the course of interrogation upon the precise objectives of the 10th MAS post-occupational network. Nothing has been adduced which would indicate that the groups, as far as Subject is concerned, were designed for a post-defeat mission. From a general standpoint this program would seem hardly likely to be undertaken by Subject in view of the fact that he had so completely compromised himself in the service of the Germans and the German Intelligence System, and therefore knew that all members of his Units would be removed form circulation either by Allied or Italian agencies.
Recommendation:
Subject states that Mario Rossi, on Subject's orders, if necessary, could effectively apprehend all members of the network and uncover their arms and explosives cache. Further recommendation in this regard will be rendered following receipt of preliminary interrogation of Mario ROSSI. Interrogation conducted and report written by Raymond G. Rocca of this Unit. (TNA WO204/12803)

Angleton signed the report and copies were sent to G-2(Ib) 15th Army Group; the AC of S, G-2, CI, 5th Army (Nichols); IV Corps, G-2, CI; SCI/Z/Genoa and SCI/Z/Milan.

It will be noted that in Rossi's interrogation report, he stated that 'at least a large part of the explosives were hidden near SORI' and that he understood 'that they were found and seized by the Partisans.' This suggests that other parts of the cache remained hidden. Whether the partisans located them or Rossi arranged for the authorities to retrieve them is unknown.

Borghese made references to the arrangements he made with Otto Begus, a German SS officer who ran a team which trained Fascist Italians for stay-behind sabotage and espionage missions. An account of the training and the outcome of those who volunteered can be found in Volume IV of *Destroying Hitler's R-*

Netz. In summary, the majority were apprehended at checkpoints and their interrogations included denouncements, not just of the Germans but the other Italian collaborators and the location and removal of the caches of explosives and sabotage material.

He claimed to have discussed with Rahn and Wolff about Germany's peaceful departure from Italy. Wolff claimed to have given orders to the Wehrmacht and SS that there would be no demolitions. The Navy had plans to demolish the port of Genoa and act on German instructions. He suggested putting it out of action for a period. Harster told him that Admiral Doenitz had ordered Geno to be put out of action, provided there was no interference from the Partisans.

Borghese claimed that he had previously ordered Capitano di Corvetta Arillo of the X MAS at Genoa to prepare to neutralise any demolitions and await orders. Gamma men were standing ready to swim to the submarine electric cable connecting the charges with the demolition control, and to cut it when ordered. These counter-sabotage measures had been undertaken in understanding with the local CLN. He claimed that he had instructed Rossi to give the same orders to the group headed by Mantini.

June 1945

By early June, Mario Scarpa, another X MAS agent, had been captured and interrogated.

PRELIMINARY INTERROGATION REPORT
OF SUSPECTED ENEMY AGENT
Date: 2 June 45   47 PORT SECURITY SECTION
Time: 1000 hours   CMF 15 AG
Place.: VENICE
I. Personal Particulars.
SCARPA Mario di Spiridione. Alias ROSSI Carlo.
Army agents list number 5510.
Born: PORT SAID, 21/2/24.
Residence: Avenue Forat 10, (Familiy interned), PORT SAID.
II. Circumstances of Arrest.
    Found travelling under false name (ROSSI) in company of SPERBER Rodolfo (No. 5202). Latter was traced through control of residents in hotels. Arrested 11:00 PM 31/5/45 Alberge Astoria VENICE.
III. Employers.
Gamma Operator. 10 Flot. MAS. VALDAGNO.
IV. Missions.
None, according to subject.
V. Method of Entry into Allied Territory.
Gives following information about listed agents (10 Flot). Confirmed by SPERBER Rodolfo.
    PARIGI Ezio – Agent's List 805 – Killed by partisans.
    REGNI Enzo - Agent's List 807. Home in SPEZIA.
    FABRI Walter - Agent's List 5199 - In home in PESCARA.
    GOBBI Guelf - Agent's List 5204 - In home in PESCARA.
    SISA Giorgio – Agent's List 5303 – In home in PESCARA.
    ANGELINI Giorgio - Agent's List 5509 - In home at TRIESTE.
    TABRINI Camilo - Agent's List 5159 - Stated to be working with Royal Navy at VENICE. [This entry was crossed out.]
    WOLNER Roberto – Agents List 5567 – Staying in MILAN.

WOLNER Enrico – Agents List 5508 – Left VALDAGNO to join brother in MILAN 29 May 45.

Many 10 Flot Mas members in hiding in civilian houses at VALDAGNO.

VII. Possessions.

Nothing of interest.

VIII. Interrogator's Comments.

Subject is of very little interest (CI). Grandfather English. Very contemptuous of his own people. Expresses sincere desire to be put to work outside Italy. His bearing is that of a prisoner of war and it is suggested that he be treated as such.

IX. Present Status.

Detention Centre VENICE. (Ibid.)

Although Sperber and Scarpa's reports were stated to have been forwarded to AFHQ, Sperber's was not included. The note stated that 'subjects, as members of the GAMMA Group of X FLOT MAS will be evacuated through PW Channels.

There were then several undated photographs of 'enemy agents', obtained in Venice, copies of which one imagines would have been forwarded to the relevant sections to assist their apprehension.

On 7 June 1945, Sergeant G. Curran, sent the Commanding Officer of the 85 Port Security Section Intelligence Corps in Genoa, the following memorandum stamped SECRET.

Subject: Stay behind organisation of Bn. VEGA, XMAS

1. Reference reports NA/GER/712/17 and NA/GER/17A from No. 3 SCI Unit dated 24 May 45 and 31 May 45 So investigations and interrogations have now been carried out. In the man, no important new facts would appear to have been discovered.

Under paragraph E. of the first above named report it was stated that the financial cover of the organisation was a transport company managed by the Frassoni brothers.

\#

Camillo Tardini (Ibid.)

Roberto Aprile (TNA WO204/12452)

2. Whilst that is undoubtedly correct, it should also be stated that there was a second form of financial cover which took the shape of a bar, situated at Via Trente 26/28 (red) Genoa.

Via Trente 26-28, Genoa, the location of Fenzo Bartoli's bar where the X MAS Genoa group used to meet.

To manage this bar was appointed Bartoli Fenzo, funds for the purchase of the bar being supplied byTen. Di. Vascelle ROSSI, commanding Bn. VEGA through the officers of the information group Linetti and Bertucci. A total of 800,000 lire from Bn. VEGA funds is stated to have been used for the purpose of this bar. It would appear desirable to transfer the name of Bartoli the information group, therefore. The degree of implication of Bartoli in the organisation would appear to be less than that of others, for he was given the job of bartender at the request of Rossi to Linetti. Bartoli an ex Sergeant major to Rossi was given what might be called more or less dishonourable discharge from the Vega Bn. In February after refusing to do a mission into Allied occupied territory. Rossi states that Bartoli was given the post as a man who might be trusted with the management and who knew virtually nothing of the organisation or its activities: in fact to help him in the difficult situation in which he found himself after his discharge.

3. The transport company run by the Frassoni brothers appears to have accounted for almost 3,000,000 lire which Rossi supplied for the purpose. In addition he sent in late March 1800 litres of petrol and 400 of oil to them. The unused portion was later handed over by the Frassonis to the Socialist Party of Genoa. On 24 April according to the brothers, there was delivered at their garage a transmitting set, probably by Cami. They state that on learning what it was they immediately destroyed it with a hammer. The brothers insist that they had no idea what the real purpose of their organisation was come and that the only orders they had from Rossi where to come to Genoa and to set themselves up as civilians and await further orders from him. The position of the third brother Alessandro a boy of 15 1/2 years of age would appear to be little compromised: he had gone with his elder brothers to Montorfano and there had been at first without payment and then given a small allowance by the Paymaster at the Bn. Vega. He was not given any briefing whatever and when his brothers came away from Montorfano he followed them. It would seem clear that far from being a member of X Mas he was merely a mascot at Montorfano. Working with the Frassoni brothers was Angeli Alberico as a driver.

4. There joined the group of Linetti on the 15 April Ten. Prete to take over from Linetti the command of his group for disciplinary purposes. He had returned from Campalto shortly before being sent to Genoa from Montorfano from which latter place he had been absent since Sep. 44. He asked Rossi for some duty and Rossi had nothing to offer him except to report to Genoa. In view of his long absence from Montorfano and the very short space of time he spent there after his return it would appear that he knew even less than the other members of his group

about the activities of the organisation. A separate report on his activities at Campalto is being prepared.

5. Mentioned in report of No. 3SCI unit above quoted is the name of Baldo Reme. In the original allocation of personnel he was ordered to report to Turin as a radio operator. It was not possible for him to complete the journey in time to arrive before the partisan rising there. Ten Mambelli who was in charge of the group there advised him to go to Genoa and regularise his position with the Regia Marina there.

6. With regard to the arms held by the group in Genoa one part was consigned to the partisans at Seri, near Genoa: another part was given to Ten "Hans" of the partisans here at Genoa; the third part is held hidden here in Genoa in a place known only to Linetti who has offered to show where they are if given the opportunity. They include five Biretta rifles, 5 automatic Biretta pistols, a box of grenades and a box of rifle ammunition.

7. The only admissions as to knowledge of the aims of the organisation have come from Linetti, Pia?, Bartucci, and Prete. They stayed that Rossi's orders to them were to establish themselves in Genoa as civilians in general, keep themselves in touch with the central organisation at Milan and obtain the collaboration of that political party which appeared most likely to help them in their alleged object of helping to bring about the reconstruction of Italy. These members of Mantini's group who have been arrested state that all they knew of their aims was to prevent the port being destroyed by the Germans. Equally the Frassoni group and also Bartoli deny all knowledge of any long term policy.

8. The information group under Linetti left Montorfano for Genoa in early February and they Frassoni brothers about

the middle of that month. Mantini's Group however did not leave Montorfono until the 8 April.

9. No discrepancies of any importance have been discovered in the stories of the various people interrogated. In an appendix will be included a brief summary of the facts discovered from each man interrogated. As has already been pointed out the activities to be carried out by the organisation, if it functioned at all, depended on the manner in which Rossi interpreted the orders given to him by Borghese: whilst the officers of the group appear to have had little information, the other ranks had virtually none.

Appendix to report on Bn. VEGA stay behind organisation

1. Notes on points of information obtained from members of Frassoni group.

2. FRASSONI Carlo di Alfredo di Carella Ernesta born at Genoa 29.11 1916, resident at Geno Via Del Perdone 13. Sgt in X MAS since Nov 1943. Dispatched from Montorfono on 19 or 20 Feb 45 on orders of Rossi. Told to set himself up as a civilian, to take up transport business with vehicles supplied by Rossi, await arrival of Rossi. On Rossi's visit which took place in first days of March, Rossi then further [gave him] one million lire, on leaving supplied a further 2 million. On his instructions a garage was rented and two further auto cars were bought: on later instruction they bought a third auto car: denies all knowledge of real aims of organisation.

FRASSONI DIONINO brother of above resident at Corse Sardinia 80/16. Sgt in X Mas since March 1944. Orders were to collaborate with brother in carrying out instructions given to him.

FRASSONI Alessandro brother of above, resident at Via Piacenza 76a interno 11. Employed at Montorfano as general errand boy by Bn. since Nov 44: kind of mascot to Bn.

Brought away by brothers when they left; had no briefing of any kind.

ANGELI Alberico di Andrea and di Pedrocca Carolina, born at Porte Valtreavglia, province of Vareza, living provisionally at home of Frassoni Carlo, Via Del Perdone 13, Genoa. Sgt in X Mas since Feb 44. Ordered to carry out same instructions as to the older Frassoni's

like them denies all knowledge of any long term policy. None of them admit to having received the order to put transport a disposition of C.L.N.

Part group, under command of Mantini

Of this group two only have been arrested at GENOA.

ARDITO Stefano, fu Lucio and di Barteluzzi Caterina, born 23.6.1927 at Treviso, lodging in Genoa at Piazza Palermi 5/41. Has an older brother in X Maas, and it was agreed by Rossi that Stefano should be taken on at Montorfano as a general errand boy. Whilst he received uniform of member of Mas was not in fact a member as he was under age. Elder brother was chosen at first as a member of Mantini's group but as it was found that he had fascist precedent Mantini and Rossi decided that he was not a suitable member of the group and he was posted away. Whilst he was dispatched elsewhere, subject Stefano was sent to Genoa on post mission. On arrival here subject states that Mantini told him that he could not use his services owing to his extreme youth. Subject apparently knows nothing of group's activities and his story is believed.

GINI Ulisse di Ubalde and di Magnani Speranza, born at Bologna 15.6.21 living at Genoa Via Fratelli Chiarella, 11/5. Member of X Mas from 12.11.44. Send from Montorfano by Rossi on 8 April 45 under command of Mantini with the order to carry out such instructions as we're given by Mantini to prevent destruction of port by Germans. He states that Mantini told them that as soon the above mission was accomplished they would be allowed to break off all connection with X Mas. Subject states that hey at outbreak of insurrection in Genoa, he handed over all of group 21 Brigata "Mazzini". States that on 24 April was paid off by Mantini with the sum of 10,000 lire, Mantini refusing to give him more

since he had not made himself available for any action necessary as part of group at time of insurrection.
Information Group.
Linetti Giovanni di Leone and di Ferrari Teresa born at Verbani Intra, province of Nevara 8.11.21, at present living in Via Trento 2°/30 Genoa. 2 Lieut. in X Mas from 1.1.44.
Bertaccia Alde di Giacomo and di Ganessa Angela, born at Santa Margerita Ligura, Geno, 13.5.23 at present residing at Genoa Via Trento 20/30 2nd Lieut. in X Mas since Dec. 43.
Prete Antonio di Giovanni and di Caro Maria easyLatizi, born at Belzano Vicentina, Vicenza, 29.9.11; at present residing at Salita Santa Barbara 24/10. Lieut. in X Mas from Nov 43.
Linetti Bertuccio and Pia were send in charge of a group consisting of the Warrant Officer, 3 NCOs [Non Commissioned Officers] and one other rank from Montorfano by Rossi in early Feb 45: Linetti was at that time in charge, and was instructed to pay sum equivalent to six months pay to all members of group. Orders were to set themselves up as civilians, to keep in touch by radio with centre of organisation at Milan, to await later orders from Rossi, and to associate themselves with Comitate di Liberazione, after liberation of Italy. They never got any detailed orders from Rossi, according to Linetti. Pia was to set himself up not in general itself but at Pieve Ligure, and to keep in touch with Linetti.
Prete (see separate interrogation) was sent to take over command of group from Linetti in last few days preceding insurrection in Genoa.

Subsidiary financial cover.
Barteli Fenzo di Nelle and di Fini Annunciata born at San Marcello Pisteieze, Province of Pisteis, 28.6.1917, residing at Westea, [sic], Via Francese Pezze 12/17. 2 de case in X Mas from Dec 43, but this charged ask from Feb 45. On discharge was given a personal mission on behalf of Rossi and later on request of Rossi was placed in charge of management of bar bought in name of Barteli but out of funds supplied for groups of organisation set up in Genoa Via Trente 26/28 (red). States that he thought that the money was supplied by Rossi personally possibly to provide a livelihood for Rossi

after occupation of Italy by Allies. Denies all knowledge of organisation and its aims.

Other Arrest.

Baldo Roma di N.N. and di Baldo Amelisbern at Padua 11.6.1818. At present resident in Via Casa Regio 24/6. De cape R/T in X Mas since March 44. Destined for group at Turin but arrived after outbreak of insurrection and was sent to Genoa by his officer Mambelli with order to regularise his position with the Regia Marina there. Denies all knowledge of functions of group at Turin and still less if possible of those at Genoa. (TNA WO204/12453)

In the Weekly Counter-Intelligence Sitrep [Situation Report] of the 15th Army Group dated 11 June 1945 it stated:

'10 members NP Bn 10 FLOTMAS also identified or arrested. [Nuotatori – Paracadutisti was a battalion of trained swimmers and parachutists.] Of the 400 X MAS men stationed in Screening at Army cages and further enquiries BOLZANO MERANO areas continue.' (Ibid.)

The following day, another sitrep was submitted:

NATALE PANCALDI

As a result of leads obtained from the capture of four members of the Prince BORGHESE underground organisation, a fifth member of the group was also arrested. The capture of the a/m [above mentioned], a former seaman of the X Flottiglia MAS, concludes the roundup of all the members of the group, was said to have gone to rejoin his family in TORINO DI SANGRO, province of CHIETI.' (Ibid.)

There was then a handwritten report giving details of Lt. Camilo Tadini, another X MAS agent.

TADINI.   Camilo.   (A).

                                    [Surname &
                                     Country] : ITALY

                        Profession : Naval Engineer.
12-44. P.2 C.I. - X. Flotilla MAS. Maybe Genoese Speedboat
                     with Mission allied targets. Last seen
                     Valdagno. June '44. (May now be
                     at Portofino.)   File 704

                     5'5". brown hair, Cleanshaven
                     very good white teeth, athletic built not-
                     heavy build, very energetic, From
                     Venice.

26. Oct' 44. R.N. Leghorn.   In Gibraltar Diano attack 2-3
                   [?]   august 1943. Believed now   Ref.
                             with Republican Fascists.   50203/450

(Ibid.)

On 15 June, 1st Lt. Alvin C. Leone of the CIC forwarded
information about Alberto Luciani to the Headquarters of the A.C.
of S., G-2 (CI).

1. Information has been received that subject is a member of
   the X Flotilla MAS underground organization in
   BOLOGNA and MODENA.
2. Interrogation of captured members of this group has
   revealed that subject, the radio operator for the group, left
   BOLOGNA on 23 or 24 April to visit his family at
   TORINO di SANGRO, Province of CHIETI.
3. Subject is described as follows: Age 45-50 years; grey hair;
   height about 5'5"; blue eyes; normal build.
4. It is recommended that the above information be
   forwarded to the appropriate counter-intelligence agency
   having jurisdiction on TORINO di SANGRO.

On 16 June, Springarn sent the Acting Chief of Staff of G-2 (CI), the Counter Intelligence Section of the Fifth Army the following note. Each page had SECRET stamped in blue on the top or bottom.

1. Transmitted herewith are five Fifth Army CIC reports on the following members of the Bologna-Modena center of the X Flotilla MAS post=occupational underground movement:
   a) CUCCHIARA Elio, C.O. (Commanding Officer) of the Bologna group.
   b) CENACCHI Augusto, 2 i/c (second in charge) of the Bologna group.
   c) PANCALDI Natale
   d) RIZZOLI Carlo
   e) BONACINI Walter

2. The capture of this group represents a roundup of all the members of the underground organization thought to be in Bologna or Modena. It is believed that this capture is of substantial long-range counterintelligence importance, Because of the serious implications of this movement. The organisation was "patriotic" and nationalistic in basis, owing nothing to German support, and being basically opposed to all foreign influences in Italy. The personnel of the group who were apprehended by this Detachment with people of a much higher type than those usually found among the agents that the Germans were able to recruit for intelligence operations against the Allies. Intelligent, resourceful, and the specially trained fighters, motivated by an intense nationalism and great respect for Prince BORGHESE, the commander of the X Flotilla MAS, this group offers a general programme that would appeal to many elements of Italian society, to wealthy, influential and conservative persons, to soldiers and former soldiers, and

to ambitious and enterprising youths desirous of establishing a new and strong Italy. Their political programme of watchful waiting and joining forces with political parties which they could use for their own purposes promised then a large group of followers at the opportune time. The anti-communist programme made use of a deeply implanted fear of communism among many elements of the Italian people, which has been strengthened by years of fascist propaganda.. Their republicanism made use not only of the anti-monarchical propaganda implanted by the Republic and fascists, but also of the general dissatisfaction with the monarchy that exists among almost all parties and in great masses of Italian society. In short, the movement contained all of the seeds of a new fascism in Italy, and its members were ready, willing, and equipped to take forceful action to establish their program.

3. It is recommended that all five members of this group be interned for the duration of the World War. It is doubted whether further detailed interrogation would be of substantial value.

HEADQUARTERS
COUNTER INTELLIGENCE CORPS, FIFTH ARMY
(305TH CIC DETACHMENT)
APO 464 Section B: 11 June 1945
SUBJECT: CUCCHIARA Elio fu Tommaso, Captured Stay-behind Agent of X Flotilla MAS Underground Movement.
TO: A.C. of S. [Acting Chief of Staff], G-2(CI), Fifth Army. A.P.O. U.S. Army.

1. Reference is made to letter, HQ 15th Army Group, to G-2(CI), Fifth Army, reference. 1402/24/GSI(b)[General Staff Intelligence (Counter-Intelligence)] dated 23 May 1945, Subject: "Underground Movements", which transmitted information regarding the Bologna group of the X Flotilla MAS underground movement established by Prince BORGHESE from personnel of the 10th Flotilla MAS, and which directed that members of this group be apprehended

and detained. Reference is also made to letter, No. 3 SCI, Milan, dated 25 May 1945, file ref. NAM 712/A/3, Subject: "10th MAS Flotilla", which transmitted further information regarding the 10th Flotilla MAS stay-behind organisation, and which listed Subject's name, together with the names of five other members of the Bologna group.

2. Circumstances of Arrest:
During the course of the "S Force" operation in Bologna, Special Agents Burkel and De Rubeis This detachment uncovered information that subject was a member of the X Flotilla MAS and had possibly set up a clandestine W/T set in Bologna. Subjects mother was located and interrogated, but she stated that she had not seen him for three or four months and did not know his present whereabouts. She delivered the keys to subject's apartment at Via Marc Antonio Raimondi 21, third floor, Bologna to Agents Burkel and De Rubeis. A search revealed only various photographs of Subject, his PNF membership card, and a copy of the 31 August 1942 issue of "L'ALA D'ITALIA", which carried a picture of Subject and other persons in connection with an article on parachute training. Other occupants of the building at Via Marc Antonio Raimondi 21, Bologna, were questioned, but stated that they had not seen Subject on the premises in recent months, and could give no information as to his whereabouts.
In accordance with information received in the letters referred to in paragraph 1 of this letter, Bologna Section, CIC, 5th Army, conducted investigation of the X Flotilla MAS stay-behind group in Bologna. On 7 June 1945, CENACCHI Augusto di Luigi, another member of the Bologna stay-behind group, was apprehended by the Bologna Section, CIC 5th Army. CENACCHI stated that subject was living at Via Monte Sabotino 34, Medina. Subjects address was immediately communicated to Modena section, CIC, 5th Army, which apprehended Subject on the evening of 7 of June1945. On 8 June 1945, subject was transferred to the custody of Bologna section, CIC, 5th Army. Results of interrogation of Subject by Special Agent Richardson of this Detachment are incorporated below:

3. Personal Particulars:
Name: CUCCHIARA Elio
Alias: None.
Cover Name: None
X Flotilla MAS Group. No. 87
Birth: 19 December 1919 at Modena.
Father: CUCCHIARI Tommaso (deceased)
Mother: MANGONI Annunziata nei CUCCHIARA, resident at Via Marc'Antonio Raimondi 21, Bologna.
Occupation: Fencing Instructor.
Brother: CUCCHIARA Enio, born 9 June 1914 at Arezzo, prisoner in Germany since 8 September 1943. Subject has no other brothers or sisters.
Address: Via Monte Sabotino 34, Modena.
Marital Status: Subject is married to BUONGIORNO Italia, born 26 March 1911 at Modena, presently resident at Via Monte Sabotino 34, Modena. Subject has two children, Vittorio and Bruno, nine and six years of age respectively.
Religion: Catholic.
Nationality: Italian.
Political Background: Subject stated that he had never joined the PNF or PMF, no had held any posts or honest in the PNF or PRN (membership card attached to original copy of this report found in subjects apartment in Bologna reveals that he was inscribed in the PNF on 2 October 1935,)
Military History: Subject entered military service on 21 May 1928 as an Allievo Ufficiale in Engineering. In 1936 he became a 2nd Lt. as a Maestro di Scherma, and in 1941 lieutenant instructor in parachute training. On 9 October 1943, he was placed in a concentration camp at Rome by the Germans. On 11th November 1943 cover he was released from the concentration camp and he thereupon enrolled in the X Flotilla MAS at La Spezia as a lieutenant. Subject served as an instructor of parachute training in the NP Battalion until April 1944, receiving on that date approximately 8 months leave for reasons of health will stop in October 1944 Subject was assigned to the Vega Battalion at Montorfano, Province of Como. He received another six months leave from the end of October 1944 until 9 April 1945. He was then released from service will stop subject had been made head of the

Bologna group of the X Flotilla MAS underground movement, in February 1945.

4. Recruitment into 10th MAS Flotilla Underground Movement.

At the end of February 1945, Subject was called to the office of Captain ROSSI Mario at Montorfano, Province of Como. Captain ROSSI explained to Subject that with the end of the war in Europe many disbanded Italian soldiers and former Italian prisoners of war would be returning to the homes, without work, and without any organisation to direct them in the work of rebuilding Italy. These men would come if not taken in hand, the strongly attracted by the Communist movement. To avoid such an eventuality, it was necessary to create an organisation which could unite and direct these former military personnel. Although military personnel were those particularly to be organised, labourers and other civilians could also be enrolled. The X Flotilla MAS Was this to create a centralised and unified organisation throughout Italy with the primary aims of combating communism particularly, and fascism, and to support a political party of the centre or right will stop the organisation was not to create a political party of its own. According to Subject, Captain ROSSI did not speak of hostile acts against the allies, know of capturing the Italian government by a coup d'etat. Arms were to be given to members of the underground movement for the purpose of implementing their aid to anti-Communist elements. The movement was to organise during the period of Allied occupation, but was not to begin extensive overt activity until the departure of the Allies. A meat occasion of this conversation with Captain ROSSI, Subject accepted the propositions outlined by Captain ROSSI, and agreed to be the commanding officer of the Bologna group.

5. Training:

Subject received no formal training, but was told to faithful to the ideals of the 10th MAS Flotilla.

6. Mission:

Subjects mission was to organise and unite new members drawn principally from the ranks of disbanded soldiers and ex-POWs. Was to carry on propaganda against the Communists and in favour of the efforts being made by the X Flotilla MAS. Subject was also to make contact with centrist or rightist parties and support them by force if necessary against communist elements, infiltrating these parties with former members of the X Flotilla MAS and with new recruits of the movement.

7. Employers:

Subject knew that Captain ROSSI commander of the Vega Battalion, X Flotilla MAS, as leader of the movement, but supposed that Prince BORGHESE Valerio would, as Captain ROSSI's Superior, be perhaps the leader of the movement. Subject received four months advance pay on his military salary. He was, in addition, given approximately 900,000 lire by Lt. GOZZI for the expenses of the group.

8. Means of Identification:

Subject was given the number 87 but was not told why nor how it should be used. He was given no other means of identification.

9. Means of Communication:

Subject was to transmit information by radio in urgent cases, or otherwise by letter or persons, regarding the progress of the efforts of the Bologna group, their needs etc. He stated that he had not been asked to send political information or information regarding the allies, and that this subject was not touched upon by Captain ROSSI.

10. Subsequent Activities:

A few days after accepting leadership of the Bologna group of the X Flotilla MAS underground movement at the end of March 1945, Subject, together with RIZZOLI Carlo, and another captured member of the Bologna group, returned to Modena. Subject then remained at home in Modena, but made one trip to Milan on the second or third of April 1945 with PANCALDI Natale, where he purchased a supply of women's wear and shoes, which was transported to the home of PANCALDI in Bologna. This merchandise was to be used as an investment for the group. On 23 April 1945 Subject established contact with Major PINETTI Medardo of the Partito d'Azione of Modena. Subject explained his views to PINETTI, stated that he had a few men and arms, that he wished to place them at the disposition of Major PINETTI, and that he was under general orders from Captain ROSSI to act in such a manner. Subject explained to Major PINETTI something of the background of the movement to which he belonged. Major PINETTI Accepted subjects proposition to place at his disposition, arms and support. Subject engaged in no other organisational or propaganda activity.

11. Other Agents and Contacts:
(See paragraph 11, letter, CIC, 5th Army, to A.C. of S., G-2(CI), 5th Army, dated 9 June 1945, Subject: "CENACCHI Augusto di Luigi, Captured Stay-behind Agent of X Flotilla MAS Underground Movement".

12. Possessions:
Subject's money and documents accompany him.

13. Interrogator's Comments:
Subject appeared to cooperate quite well during interrogation. However, he denied that the movement was clandestine or hostile to the Allies, although this was admitted by 2nd Lt. BONACINI, another member of the Bologna group. The interrogators impression is that the X Flotilla MAS underground movement is in fact a clandestine armed organisation, anti-Communist and also anti-Allied in nature, capable of acts of violence in carrying out its aims. The movement appears to have been hastily organised will stop Subject did not seem to be very clear in his own mind concerning the aims or

structure of the organisation. He appears, however, to be a capable and determined leader who intended to carry out the orders of his superiors in the movement.

14. Present Status:
Subject has been placed in the Riformatoria Minorenni, Bologna, pending disposition from higher headquarters. It is recommended that he be interned.

HEADQUARTERS
COUNTER INTELLIGENCE CORPS, FIFTH ARMY
(305TH CIC DETACHMENT)
APO 464 Section B: 9 June 1945
SUBJECT: CENACCHI Augusto di Luigi, Captured Stay-behind Agent of X Flotilla MAS Underground Movement.
TO: A.C. of S., G-2 (CI), Fifth Army.
1. Reference is made to letter, HQ 15th Army Group, to G-2(CI), Fifth Army, reference. 1402/24/GSI(b) dated 23 May 1945, Subject: "Underground Movements", which transmitted information regarding the Bologna group of an underground movement established by Prince BORGHESE from personnel of the 10th MAS Flotilla, and which directed that members of this group be apprehended and detained. Reference is made to letter, No. 3 SCI, Milan, dated 25 May 1945, file ref. NAM 712/A/3, Subject: "10th MAS Flotilla", which transmitted further information regarding the 10th Flotilla MAS stay-behind organisation, and which listed Subject's name, together with the names of five other members of the Bologna group., directing that the necessary investigation be made in Bologna.

2. Circumstances of Arrest:
In accordance with information received in the letters referred to in paragraph 1 of this letter, Bologna Section, CIC, 5th Army, initiated investigation of the 10th MAS Flotilla stay-behind group in Bologna. On 7 June 1945, the Anagrafico Office in Bologna was checked where it was found that a CENACCHI Augusto lived at Strada Maggiore 54, Bologna. Subsequent to contact made with the family of CENACCHI

Augusto he presented himself at the Bologna Office of this Detachment and at approximately 1830 hours on 7 June 1945 confessed to Special Agent Frank A. Messina that he was a member of the Bologna stay-behind group of the X Flotilla MAS underground movement. Interrogation of Subject by Special Agent Messina revealed the following information:

3. Personal Particulars:
Name: CENACCHI Augusto
Alias: None.
Cover Name: None
X Flotilla MAS Group. No. 91
Birth: 23 August 1924 at Bologna
Father: CENACCHI Luigi, Strada Maggiore 54, Bologna.
Mother: MARZI Fernanda, Strada Maggiore 54, Bologna.
Address: Strada Maggiore 54, Bologna.
Marital Status: Single.
Religion: Catholic.
Nationality: Italian.
Political Background: Subject was inscribed in the usual Fascist youth organisations, and has had no other Fascist affiliations.
Military History: Subject entered military service on 25 November 1943 at Bologna, and was assigned to the 15th Coast Defense Battalion at Modena. On 20 December 1943, Subject was transferred to the Aeronautic Parachutist group at Tradate, Province of Varese. He attended a school for parachutists and made his first jump on 24 April 1944. On the following day, subject was sent to Castell Ritaldi, Province of Spolleto, together with his company, and while there his company became a part of the Folgore Regiment. On 11 June 1944, the company withdrew and went to Angera, Province of Varese, and became a part of the "Azzuro" Battalion. The Battalion went to Cannobio, province of Novara, the end of September 1944, and took part in action against the Partisans. On 27 or 28 October 1944, the Battalion returned to Tradate. Subject heard that the Battalion would be used another time against the Partisans, and not wishing to participate, he deserted. Subject presented himself for enrollment in the X

Flotilla MAS on 8 November 1944, at Montorfano, Province of Como. He was assigned to the Vega battalion and remained with this unit until 22 March 1945, when he returned to his home in Bologna.

4. Recruitment into 10th MAS Flotilla Underground Movement.

About the 1st of February 1945, subject was called to the private room of his company commander, Lt. CUCCHIARA, and was asked if he was disposed to be part of a movement that was striving for the following purposes: a free and independent Italy, without Fascism, without Communism, without the Germans, and without any other party that would take away the liberty of Italy. CUCCHIARA explained that this movement was being organised by Prince Valerio BORGHESE, commander of the X Flotilla MAS, and that the Vega Battalion had the mission of initiating it. CUCCHIARA further explained that small groups of this movement were being formed in several of the principle cities, such as Milan, Turin, Genova, Venice, and Bologna. The Lieutenant said that he was going to head the Bologna group which would consist of six men, and if Subject joined the movement, he would be assigned to this group so that he could also be near his home.

5. Training:

Subject received no formal training. He was told to spread propaganda and explain his ideas of a free and independent Italy to all the young men with whom he came in contact.

6. Mission:

This movement was supposed to begin after the Allies left Italy. Subject's mission was to Organise the Italian youths and disbanded soldiers and to carry on propaganda against the Communists. The X Flotilla MAS movement was to support the rightist groups and to use force, if necessary, against the Communists. Subject stated that there had not been any mention made of the Allies because it was not known what policy the allies would adopt in Italy. However, the movement was organised to give opposition to any party and any power which attempted to interfere with Italian liberty and independence.

7. Employers:
Subject's Superior in the Bologna group was Lt. CUCCHIARA. The Bologna group was dependent on Capt. ROSSI Mario, of Milan and the leader of the 10th Flotilla MAS movement was Prince Valerio BORGHESE.

8. Means of Identification:
all the members were given a different number, but subject is not sure if this was to be used as a means of identification. Subject states that all members of the X Flotilla MAS knew each other and there was no need for having any special means of identification. Subject was given No. 91.

9. Means of Communication:
All information was to be transmitted by radio to the central headquarters at Milan. There was also a liaison group consisting of captain LO CASCIO, 2nd L. SESSA, and seaman VISCONTINI, who would travel by car and contact all the groups in the various cities.

10. Subsequent Activities:
Subject left the X Flotilla MAS at Montorfano, Province of Como, on 20 March 1945, and returned to his home in Bologna. He was supposed to have received six months' advanced pay at the rate of 5,500 lire a month, But received only about 14,000 in all. He was, he to be included in the use Of approximately 900,000 lire given to Lt. CUCCHIARA by Lt. GOZZI for the expenses of the group. When Subject returned to Bologna he resumed his private life and began to engage in private business.

11. Other Agents and Contacts:
The X Flotilla MAS movement was organised in the following manner:

Organisation of Movement in Milan.
ROSSI Mario, Captain (arrested)
LO CASCIO Vincenzo, Captain, 30-35 years; 1.73m; robust; round face; was captured by Partisans in April 1945, but outcome unknown. [The name and details would have been sent to the Field Security Units who manned the checkpoints to help them identify them should they attempt to cross from enemy to Allied occupied territory.]
VENUTA Antonio, 2nd Lt. was in charge of motor pool (arrested).
SESSA Vincenzo, 2nd Lt.; liaison officer (arrested).
VISCONTINI Giangaleazzo, Seaman; his sister Antoinette is engaged to Captain LO CASCIO; lives in Verese; 21 years; 1.73m; well-built; dark chestnut hair; brown eyes; engineering student in Milan.
SOLARI (Umberto?), Maresciallo; 28-30 years; 1.74m; slender; black hair; brown eyes; small moustache; believed to have been killed.
MERELLO Carlo, Seaman; cousin of Captain ROSSI; about 21 years; 1.77m; lender; slight stoop; bites fingernails; Brown hair; lives in Genoa or in a town near there.
TIRELLI Luigi, Seaman; (arrested).
LANGIU Antonio, Sergeant (arrested).
LANGIU (fnu) Seaman (arrested).
ROSSETTO Sergio, Sergeant (arrested).
CAPRA Mario, 2nd Lt. (arrested).
FERRETTO (fnu) Seaman; worked with CAPRA.

Organisation of Movement in Turin:
MAMBELLI Edmondo, 2nd Lt., Chief of the Turin group; lived at Inverigo, Province of Milan, but wanted to move to Val d'Intelvi, Province of Como; 46 years; 1.68m;; grey hair; Regular build; brown eyes; native of Forli.

PARI Elio, Seaman; About 24 years; 1.74m; well built; black wavy hair; from Rome area.
ELLI Ennio, Seaman; About 22 years; was private secretary of Lt. GOZZI and also gained the confidence of Captain ROSSI. He had access to funds of the battalion and miss appropriated more than 200,000 lire for which he was arrested by his unit around the 1st of March 1945, and taken to a gaol in Turin. He was later released by the Partisans and returned to Milan.

Organisation of Movement in Genoa
LINETTI Giovanni, 2nd Lt. (arrested).DOGA Pietro, Seaman.
VIAN (fnu), Seaman; about 20-3 years; 1.70m; dark kinky hair; possibly from Cremona.
RIGHETTO Bruno, Seaman; about 24 years; pugilist; 1.66m; heavy set shoulders; wavye black hair.
FRASSONI Carlo, Sergeant; (arrested).
FRASSONI Dionino, Sergeant; (arrested).
ANGELI Federico, Sergeant (arrested).

Organisation of Group in Venice:
VERSINI Ricardo, Sergeant Major; About 35 years of age; 1.77m; athletic build; small moustache; dark chestnut hair; believed to have a small scar on face which he received years ago; from Venice.
GRASSO Rino; Sergeant Major; About 35 years old; high receding forehead; very thin black hair; almost bald; 1.72m; very slender.
FABRO Piero, Seaman; About 21 years old; 1.72m; straight blonde hair; fairly well built; is a native of Venice and has family there. (Ibid.)

In addition to the above groups, there was another group, the location of which is unknown to subject, headed by 2nd Lt. MANTINI and 2nd Lt. GIULIANI, With approximately 30 men under them.

MANTINI Giuseppi, 2nd Lt.; 32 years old; robust build; slightly near sighted; black straight hair; of Abruzzese origin. GIULIANI Giuliano, 2nd Lt. 25 years old; well-built; black straight hair; from Liguria; last seen in March 1945 in the hospital at Como. PERNECHELE Guido, Sergeant Major; 25 years old; 1.73m; robust; comes from Turin. LEGOVINI Marcello, Sergeant; 24 years old; very slender; small moustache; chestnut hair.

12. Possessions:

Subject's money and documents accompany him.

13. Interrogator's Comments:

Subject appears to be a high type of person and rather idealistic in sentiments. He showed complete willingness to cooperate fully during interrogation and was able to furnish considerable information on other agents and contacts. Subject frankly admitted that they X Flotilla MAS movement was clandestine in nature and hostile to the Communists and to any power, foreign or domestic, that tended to deprive the Italians of their freedom and independence. This last statement might be construed as indicating hostility to the Allies, but it is the interrogator's opinion that subject is satisfied with the Allies' policy in Italy, and even desires a continuance of allied occupation in Italy, at least until a strong central government has been set up that can maintain law and order throughout the country.

14. Present Status:

Subject has been placed in the Riformatoria Minorenni, Bologna, pending disposition from higher headquarters. It is recommended that he be interned.

HEADQUARTERS
COUNTER INTELLIGENCE CORPS, FIFTH ARMY
(305TH CIC DETACHMENT)
APO 464 Section B:lwf 11 June 1945

SUBJECT: PANCALDI Natale di Romelo, Captured Stay-behind Agent of X Flotilla MAS Underground Movement. TO: A.C.of S., G-2 (CI), Fifth Army. Reference is made to letter, HQ 15th Army Group, to G-2(CI), Fifth Army, reference. 1402/24/GSI(b) dated 23 May 1945, Subject: "Underground Movements", which transmitted information regarding the Bologna group of an underground movement established by Prince BORGHESE from personnel of the X Flotilla MAS, and which directed that members of this group be apprehended and detained. Reference is made to letter, No. 3 SCI, Milan, dated 25 May 1945, file ref. NAM 712/A/3, Subject: "10th MAS Flotilla", which transmitted further information regarding the X Flotilla MAS stay-behind organisation, and which listed subject's name, together with the names of five other members of the Bologna group.

2. Circumstances of Arrest:
In accordance with information received in the letters referred to in paragraph 1 of this letter, Bologna Section, CIC, 5th Army, initiated investigation of the X Flotilla MAS stay-behind group in Bologna. On 7 June 1945, Augusto di Luigi, another member of the Bologna stay-behind group, was apprehended by the Bologna Section, CIC, 5th army. CENACCHI identified Subject as a member of the group and stated that subject lived in Bologna, at Via Irnerio 17. A call was made by Special Agent Messina of the Bologna section of this department at the home of Subject on 8 June 1945, but Subject was not present, and the family stated that Subject had gone to Florence on business two days previously. Subjects father assured Special Agent Messina that he would go to Florence and bring back his son. On 11 June 1945 at approximately 1000 hours, Subject and his father presented themselves at the office of the Bologna Section, CIC, 5th Army. Results of interrogation of Subject by Special Agent Messina of this detachment are incorporated below:

3. Personal Particulars:
Name: PANCALDI Natale.

Alias: None.
Cover Name: None
X Flotilla MAS Group. No. 92.
Birth: 31 August 1924 at Bologna.
Father: PANCALDI Romolo, resident at Via Irnerio 17, Bologna.
Mother: TOLOMELLI, Vittoria, resident at Via Irnerio 17, Bologna.
Brother: PANCALDI, Giancarlo, resident at Via Irnerio 17, Bologna.
Sisters: None.
Address: Via Irnerio 17, Bologna.
Marital Status: Single.
Religion: Catholic.
Nationality: Italian.
Political Background: Subject belonged to the usual Fascist youth organisations but has had no other Fascist affiliations.
Military History: Subject entered military service on 15 March 1943 at Prione, province of Pola, at the Naval Academy there, to take a course as a naval officer. He remained there until eight September 1943, and was then taken prisoner by the Germans and taken to a concentration camp near Pola, where he remained until 6 October 1943. Subject escaped from the concentration camp after a month of hiding in the mountains, he managed to escape to his home in Bologna in November 1943. On 6 January 1945 Subject was arrested at LANZO Intelvi, Province of Como, by members of the X Flotilla MAS God because he had illegally bought gasoline from them. He was held in prison almost a month. On 31st January 1945, Captain ROSSI, commander of the Vega battalion of the X Flotilla MAS, told Subject that he would either join the ranks of the X Flotilla MAS all be sent to Innsbruck as a prisoner. Subject stated that he accepted enrollment in the X Flotilla MAS and that he was held as a semi-prisoner. On 20 March 1945, Subject left his unit at Montorfano and went to his home in Bologna.

4. <u>Recruitment into X Flotilla MAS Stay-behind Movement.</u>
About 25 February 1945, Subject was called to the office of his company commander, Lt. CUCCHIARA, and was asked if

he wanted to return to Bologna. CUCCHIARA explained that the X Flotilla MAS was organising a movement that was directed against the communists, the fascists and the Germans, and in fact a movement that would be against any totalitarian form of government. Lt. CUCCHARIA stated that if PANCALDI Joined this movement, he would be assigned to the Bologna group and this would be stationed at home with his family. Lt. CUCCHIARA also said that the Bologna group would contact the CLN of that city and try to work in harmony with it. Captain ROSSI was against having PANCALDI in the movement because he feared that Subject might betray them, but Lt. CUCCHIARA vouched for him.

5. Training:
   Subject received no formal training. Lt. CUCCHIARA told Subject that he would receive instructions when they arrived in Bologna.

6. Mission:
   Subject did not receive any specific mission - he was told that he would receive his instructions after he returned to his home in Bologna subject was made accountant for the Bologna group. They belong you group received approximately 900,000 lire as a working fund, which was given to Lt. CUCCHIARA by Lt. GOZZI. From this amount, 200,000 lire was spent in purchasing an automobile (Topolino) which, to save it from the Partisans was consigned by RIZZOLI Carlo on orders of Lt. CUCCHIARA to Dr. LUPO (fnu [first name unknown]) of the Prefettura of Bologna on 22 April 1945, and a motorcycle, which is still in Milan. The group also spent about 100,000 lire for transportation, and another 100,000 lire for advance payment to the group members. About 60,000 lire were given to a friend of Lt. CUCCHIARA who was going to buy merchandise for the group. When in Milan, Subject and Lt. CUCCHIARA also invested approximately 500,000 lire in women's wear and shoes, all of which is at present in Subject's home in Bologna. This merchandise was to be resold in Bologna,

and the profit was to be used for the expenses of the group. The account book which subject and Lt. CUCCHIARA kept for the group is attached to the original copy of this report and marked exhibit "A".

7. Employers:
Subject stated that Lt. CUCCHIARA was the leader of the Bologna group and that Captain ROSSI was the commander of the Vega Battalion, X Flotilla MAS, and the leader of the movement.

8. Means of Communication:
The Bologna group of the stay-behind agents were to communicate by radio with captain ROSSI, leader of the movement, in Milan. There also was to be a Courier service established by members of the Milan group.

9. Means of Identification:
Subject was given the number 92 by Lt. CUCCHIARA, but he did not know why or what purpose it was to serve. He had no other means of identification.

10. Subsequent Activities:
After recruitment in the movement, Subject continued to carry out his usual military duties at Montorfano. On 20 March 1945, Subject left Montofano with regular leave papers and returned to his home in Bologna. Subject resumed civilian activities after his return home and reopened his father's shoe factory in Bologna. On two or three April 1945, Subject went to Milan with Lt. CUCCHIARA, And returned with a supply of women's wear and shoes, which was to be used as an investment for the group.

11. Other Agents and Contacts:
(See paragraph 11, letter, CIC, 5th Army, to A.C. of S., G-2(CI), 5th Army, dated 9 June 1945, Subject: "CENACCHI Augusto di Luigi, Captured Stay-behind Agent of X flotilla MAS Underground Movement".
12. Possessions:

Subject's money and documents accompany him.

13. Interrogator's Comments:

Subject appears have enrolled in the Vega Battalion, X Flotilla MAS, Through compulsion rather than through preference to avoid being sent to Germany as a prisoner. He seemed quite anxious and willing to cooperate during interrogation and voluntarily furnished information which had not been specifically requested. Lt. CUCCHIARA testified that Subject did not have intentions hostile to allied interests and entered the X Flotilla MAS Movement Only as a means of returning to his home.

14. Present Status:

Subject has been placed in the Riformatoria Minorenni, Bologna, pending disposition from higher headquarters. It is recommended that he be interned.

HEADQUARTERS
COUNTER INTELLIGENCE CORPS, FIFTH ARMY
(305TH CIC DETACHMENT)
APO 464 Section B: 10 June 1945
SUBJECT: RIZZOLI Carlo fu Luigi, Captured Stay-behind Agent of 10th MAS Flotilla Underground Movement.

TO: A.C. of S., G-2 (CI), Fifth Army. APO 464 U.S. Army.
1. Reference is made to letter, HQ 15th Army Group, to G-2(CI), Fifth Army, reference. 1402/24/GSI(b) dated 23 May 1945, Subject: "Underground Movements", which transmitted information regarding the Bologna group of an underground movement established by Prince BORGHESE from personnel of the 10th MAS Flotilla, and which directed that members of this group be apprehended and detained. Reference is made to letter, No. 3 SCI, Milan, dated 25 May 1945, file ref. NAM 712/A/3, Subject: "10th MAS Flotilla", which transmitted further information regarding the 10th Flotilla MAS stay-behind organisation, and which listed subject's name, together with the names of five other members of the Bologna group.
2. Circumstances of Arrest:

In accordance with information received in the letters referred to in paragraph 1 of this letter, Bologna Section, CIC, 5th Army, initiated investigation of the 10th MAS Flotilla stay-behind group in Bologna. On 7 June 1945, CENACCHI Augusto di Luigi , a member of the Bologna stay-behind group, was apprehended by the Bologna Section, CIC, 5th Army. CENACCHI identified Subject as a member of the Bologna group and stated that Subject lived in Bologna at Via garibaldi 4. CENACCHI also revealed that Subject had a cache of arms, ammunition, and a W/T set hidden in the elevator shaft of the building in which he lived. On the night of 7 June 1945, Special Agent Messina, accompanied by two BolognaCS Agents, went to the home of subject and apprehended him, after he had attempted to evade capture by concealing himself, in an obscure room in the elevator shaft of the building in his home. Results of interrogation by Special Agent Messina of this Detachment are incorporated below:

3. Personal Particulars:
Name: RIZZOLI Carlo
Alias: None.
Cover Name: None
X Flotilla MAS Group. No. 90
Birth: 5 November 1923 at Bologna
Father: RIZZOLI Luigi (deceased).
Mother: CAZZOLA Giuditta, Via Garibaldi 4, Bologna.
Address: Via Garibaldi 4, Bologna.
Marital Status: Single.
Religion: Catholic.
Nationality: Italian.
Political Background: Subject was inscribed in the usual Fascist youth organisations, and has had no other Fascist affiliations.
Military History: Subject entered military service on 13 January 1943 at Bologna, and was assigned to the 8th Parachute Battalion, 185th Regiment of the Nembo Division, at Tukwini, province of Viterbo. He remained with this unit until 8 September 1943, returning on that date to his home in Bologna. On 28 March 1944, subject enrolled in the 10th MAS

Flotilla at Bologna, and was sent to Iesole, Province of Venice with the NP (Nuotatore Paracadutista) Battalion. In May 1944, the Battalion was transferred to Montorfano, Province of Como, And in November 1944 its name was changed to the Vega Battalion. Subject remand with the Vega Battalion at Montorfano, leaving his unit on 15 March 1945 to return to his home in Bologna.

4. Recruitment into 10th MAS Flotilla Underground Movement.
At the end of January or the beginning of February 1945, Subject was called to the private room of his Company Commander, Lt. CUCCHIARA, and was asked if he intended to follow the Germans in their planned retreat, if he was of fascist tendencies, and if he favoured Communism, all of which questions Subject replied in the negative. CUCCHIARA asked subject if he was willing to join a movement that was being, organised by the 10th MAS Flotilla, the purpose of which was to combat all of the above mentioned tendencies, and Subject replied that he was in favour of such a program. Lr. CUCCHIARA then explained that the 10th MAS Flotilla was planning to establish a small group of men in several of the principal cities of northern Italy to form the nucleus off this movement, and that Subject would be assigned to the Bologna group because of the fact that his residence was in Bologna. CUCCHIARA stated that each group would be supplied with arms and ammunition which would be used to defend their cause in the eventuality that the communists adopted revolutionary methods. Each group would be furnished with a W/T set to keep in close contact with the central headquarters in Milan.

5. Training:
Subject received no formal training. He was told to always retain the Republican ideals of the 10th MAS Flotilla and to spread propaganda in its favor.

6. Mission:

Subject's mission was to spread propaganda for the movement and to contact and organise all those who favoured its ideals and principles so as to present a united front against the Communists. The movement was primarily directed against Communism and the members of the group were distributed arms so that they could be prepared in the eventuality that there arose an armed conflict in Italy between the right and left elements. The 10th MAS Flotilla movement was not essentially organised to gain control of the government, but rather to present organised resistance to the Communists and other elements that might attempt to gain ascendancy through violence. Subject and other members of the Bologna group were apparently to resume their normal civilian lives and were not given any colour occupation or organisation.

7. Employers:

Subject's Superior in the Bologna group was Lt. CUCCHIARA. The Bologna group was dependent on the central headquarters in Milan, which was under Capt. ROSSI Mario, Commander of the Vega Battalion of the 10th MAS Flotilla. The movement, however, was believed to be under the direction of Prince Valerio BORGHESE, commander of the 10thMAS Flotilla. Subject received five months advance pay and was to be included in the 900,000 lire given to given to Lt. CUCCHIARA by Lt. GOZZI for the expenses of the group.

8. Means of Identification:

Subject was given the number 90 by Lt. CUCCHIARA, but did not know why or what purpose it was to serve. Subject stated that all members of the 10th MAS Flotilla knew each other and there was no need for having any special means of identification.

9. Means of Communication:

The Bologna group was to communicate with central headquarters in Milan by radio, but also by courier.

10. Subsequent Activities:

After recruitment in the movement, Subject continued to carry out his usual military duties at Montorfano. On 20 March 1945, Subject left Montofano with returned to his home in Bologna, where he resumed his civilian activities. Subject was entrusted with a cache of arms and ammunition and also with a W/T set. Subject hid this equipment in a small room in the elevator shaft of the building where he resides subject stated that after the allied occupation, and the posting of the Allied proclamation against having W/T sets, he destroyed the radio and disposed of the parts. The arms and ammunition were recovered by Special Agent Messina and a list of the items is attached to the original copy of this report.

11. Other Agents and Contacts:

(See paragraph 11, letter, CIC, 5th Army, to A.C. of S., G-2(CI), 5th Army, dated 9 June 1945, Subject: "CENACCHI Augusto di Luigi, Captured Stay-behind Agent of X Flotilla MAS Underground Movement".

12. Possessions:

Subject's money and documents accompany him.

13. Interrogator's Comments:

Subject appears to be of an excitable nature and this, coupled with the manner in which he was apprehended and the fact that he had hidden the arms and ammunition, made Subject suspicious and reluctant to talk freely during the preliminary interrogation. However, Subject seemed to be relieved when he saw his commanding officer, Lt. CUCCHIARA, was also in custody and he spoke [illegible]. Subject admitted that X Flotilla MAS movement was clandestine in nature and hostile to the Communists, to the Fascists, and to the Germans, but he maintained that the movement was not in any way directed against the Allies. It did not intend to operate until the allies left Italy. Subject is rather confused as to the ideals and principles of the movement and seems to be a person more apt to be swayed by others than to think or lead on his own initiative.

14. Present Status:

Subject has been placed in the Riformatoria Minorenni, Bologna, pending disposition from higher headquarters. It is recommended that he be interned.

APPENDIX "A"

(Attached to letter, CIC, 5th Army to the A.C. of S., G-2(CI), 5th Army, dated 10 June 1945, Subject: "RIZZOLI Carlo fu Luigi, Number 90, Captured Stay-behind Agent of the 10th MAS Flotilla Underground Movement")

Arms, Ammunition and Explosives of Bologna group of 10th MAS Flotilla Underground Movement

Information received from interrogation of CANACCHI Augusto, Captured Agent Of the Bologna Group of the X Flotilla MAS Underground Movement revealed that there was a cache of arms and ammunition at the home of RIZZOLI Carlo, Via Garibaldi, Bologna. On 8 June 1945, Special Agent Messina, Accompanied by two Bologna CS Agents, proceeded to the home of RIZZOLI and recovered the above-mentioned cache. The arms and ammunition have been turned over to the 137th Ordnance Bomb Disposal Squad at Modena. A complete listing of the items recovered is as follows:

1. 4 boxes of hand grenades; each containing 72 grenades, total 288 grenades (hand grenades, model 35, Italian make).

2. 2 boxes of cartridges calibre 9)new) each box containing 2000 cartridges - total 4000 shells.

3. 6 long automatic rifles, calibre (new)

4. 5 short automatic rifles, calibre 9 (new)

5. 17 clips, long, for automatic rifle.

6. 3 small clips for automatic rifle.

7. 1 clip for a Thompson machine gun.

8. One box of explosives containing following items:

10 time clocks with complete mechanism

2 rolls of special fuse cord

5 small rolls of fuse cord

96 detonators

100 electric detonators

100 capsules [probably containing different strengths of acid which dissolved metal wire realising a spring which fired the explosive. Time pencils ranged from half an hour to several days.]

1 fuse cutter

HEADQUARTERS
COUNTER INTELLIGENCE CORPS, FIFTH ARMY
(305TH CIC DETACHMENT)
APO 464 Section B: 9 June 1945

SUBJECT: BONACINI Walter fu Armando, Captured Stay-behind Agent of X Flotilla MAS Underground Movement.

TO: A.C. of S., G-2 (CI), Fifth Army. APO U.S. Army.

1. Reference is made to letter, HQ 15th Army Group, to G-2(CI), Fifth Army, reference. 1402/24/GSI(b) dated 23 May 1945, Subject: "Underground Movements", which transmitted information regarding the Bologna group of an underground movement established by Prince BORGHESE from personnel of the 10th Flotilla, and which directed that members of this group be apprehended and detained. Reference is made to letter, No. 3 SCI, Milan, dated 25 May 1945, file ref. NAM 712/A/3, Subject: "10th MAS Flotilla", which transmitted further information regarding the 10th Flotilla MAS stay-behind organisation, and which listed subject's name, together with the names of five other members of the Bologna group.

2. Circumstances of Arrest:

In accordance with information received in the letters referred to in paragraph 1 of this letter, Bologna Section, CIC, 5th Army, initiated investigation of the 10th Flotilla MAS stay-behind group in Bologna. On 7 June 1945, CENACCHI identified Subject as a member of the group and stated that Subject lived in Modena, but was unable to give his address.

This information was immediately communicated to Modena Section, CIC, 5th Army, which apprehended Subject at his home on the morning of 8 June 1945. After he had evaded capture on the evening of the 7 June by concealing himself on the roof of his home. On 8 June 1945, Subject was transferred to the custody of Bologna Section, CIC, 5th Army. Results of interrogation of Subject by Special Agent Richardson of this Detachment are incorporated below:

3. Personal Particulars:
Name: BONACINI Walter
Alias: None.
Cover Name: None
X Flotilla MAS Group. No. 88
Birth: 19 May 1923 Modena.
Father: BONACINI Armando (deceased).
Mother: PEDRETTI Giuseppina nei BONACINI, resident at Via Calle di Lucca 28, Modena.
Brothers: None.
Sister: BONACINI Mafalda, born 2 August 1921 at Modena, resident with mother.
Marital Status: Single.
Religion: Catholic.
Nationality: Italian.
Political Background: Subject belonged to the usual Fascist youth organisations, automatically becoming a member of the PNF at the age of twenty-one. He stated that he had never held any posts or honors in the PNF or PRF, and had not become a member of the PRF.
Military Background: Subject entered military service in March 1942 the Accademia Militare Artilleria e genio, from which he graduated on 1 August 1943 with the rank of 2nd Lieutenant of the Engineers. On 8 September 1943 Subject was at his home on a month's leave. Subject enrolled in the Republican Fascist Army on 25 November 1943 with the rank of 2nd Lieutenant. He was assigned to the Primo Battaglione Genio Guastatore at Alessandria. At the end of May 1944, the Battalion was dissolved, and between May and October 1944 Subject served in the 119th Battaglione Genio Costruttore at Bologna and at Bibiena, Province of Arezzo. In October 1944 his request to

be assigned to the 10th MAS Flotilla was granted and he entered service with the 10th MAS Flotilla in that month at Turin. From Turin he was sent to Montorfano, Province of Como, where a center had been established with the principal or sole purpose of preparing a clandestine stay-behind political movement. Subject did not know precisely when the Montorfano center had been established, but was of the opinion that it had been instituted only a short time before his arrival in October 1944. He stated that there were approximately one hundred and fifty military personnel at Montorfano, but that only about 50 at the time of his stay between October 1944 and April 1945 were destined for the stay-behind movement, the other hundred personnel being stationed there to camouflage the purpose and scope of the movement. Publicly Montorfano was known as the command post of the NP Battaglione of the 10th MAS Flotilla, later in November 1944 known as the Battaglione Vega.

4. Recruitment into X Flotilla MAS Stay-behind Movement. On about 15th March 1945, Capt. ROSSI Mario, Commanding Officer of the Battaglione Vega, called six officers together in his office at Montorfano who had been designated for the stay-behind movement. Subject was one of the six. Captain ROSSI spoke of the danger of Communism and of the need of having a counter-balancing force. He conceived of the movement as republican-liberal in nature and anti-monarchical. The Allies were to be considered enemies in Italy, as Italy should be governed by Italians free from foreign domination. The stay-behind movement was to be composed principally of 10th MAS Flotilla personnel, well-organized, cohesive and armed. It was to remain clandestine until the opportune moment, that is when the leaders of the movement had found the right political party to support. No existing political party was designated as the right party, but the party chosen would be of centrist or rightist direction. The 10th MAS Flotilla would constitute the striking force of whichever party was chosen. During the presence of the Allies in Italy, the members of the movement were to carry out clandestine propaganda and organization particularly among ex-military

personnel but also among civilians. Acts of violence against the Allies were not contemplated, as the Allies were considered too strong; acts of violence would be impractical and result only in the destruction of the movement. Subject was designated as the second in command under Lt. CUCCHIARA Elio for the Bologna zone. Subject accepted the principles of the stay-behind movement and the position of second in command for the Bologna zone.

5. Training:
   Subject received no formal training.

6. Mission:
   Subject's mission was that of being second in command to Lt. CUCCHIARA Elio for the Bologna zone, engaging in propaganda and organisation for the movement, making contact with any political party of their own ideals and principles, carrying on clandestine warfare against the Communists in case of armed aggression by the Communists, and transmitting information of value or of interest to captain ROSSI. Subject under the members of the Bologna group were apparently to resume their normal civilian lives. They were not given any cover occupation or organisation.

7. Employers:
   Subject knew Capt. ROSSI, Commander of the Vega Battaglione, 10th MAS Flotilla, as the leader of the movement, but supposed that Capt. ROSSI was not acting on his own initiative put in agreement with his superior officers stop subject received four months advanced pay, and was to be included in the use of approximately 900,000 lire given to given to Lt. CUCCHIARA by Lt. GOZZI for the expenses of the group.

8. Means of Identification:
   Subject was given the number 88 by Lt. CUCCHIARA, but did not know why or what purpose it was to serve. He had no other means of identification.

9. Means of Communication:

The Bologna group of the stay-behind agents were to communicate with Captain ROSSI by radio principally, but also by mail and courier.

10. Subsequent Activities:

After recruitment in the movement, Subject continued to carry out his usual military duties in Engineering at Montorfano. On 6 April 1945, Subject left Montofano with regular leave papers and returned to his home in Modena. He engaged in no activity after his return home except that of familiarising himself with the progress of the various political parties. He carried out no propaganda or organizational work as he was awaiting orders.

11. Other Agents and Contacts:

(See paragraph 11, letter, CIC, 5th Army, to A.C. of S., G-2(CI), 5th Army, dated 9 June 1945, Subject: "CENACCHI Augusto di Luigi, Captured Stay-behind Agent of X Flotilla MAS Underground Movement".

12. Possessions:

Subject's money and documents accompany him.

13. Interrogator's Comments:

Subject appeared to cooperate quite well during interrogation. He frankly stated during interrogation that this 10th MAS Flotilla movement was clandestine in nature and hostile to Communists, the Allies, and to any other foreign power in Italy. The interrogators impression is that this 10th MAS Flotilla movement is in fact a clandestine armed organisation, anti-Communist and also anti-Allied in nature, capable of acts of violence in carrying out their aims. The movement appears to have been hastily organised. Subject does not seem to be too clear in his own mind concerning the aims of the movement. He appears, however, to be a capable and determined leader who intended to carry out the orders of his superiors in the movement.

14. Present Status:

Subject has been placed in the Riformatoria Minorenni, Bologna, pending disposition from higher headquarters. It is recommended that he be interned. (Ibid.)

Captain M. McMullen of the Intelligence Corps attached to the 85 Port Security Section, sent the G2(CI_ IV Corps, APO 304 at Genoa a further report on the X Mas stay behind subversive organisation on 19 June.

1. Herewith a general report on the above organisation as far as it concerns members arrested at GENOVA.

2. It is regretted that such a long time has elapsed before sending this since it was considered advisable to consult Captain FAIRWEATHER [Arthur Fairweather was a Canadian CIC officer] before sending it and the matter had to await his return. Internment is recommended though the extreme youth of two of its members – FRASSONI, Alessandro and ARDITO, Stefano should be taken into consideration, it is felt that they might be released and placed under house arrest at an early date.

July 1945

A memo dated 1 July stated that Frassoni and Ardito had been evacuated to Terni and placed under house arrest.

The next document was not until 14 July when 1ˢᵗ Lt. James Singleton, Commanding Officer of the SCI/Z Units in Milan, submitted the following report to the Acting Chief of Staff: -

Subject: Interrogation Report of BORDOGNA, Mario, member of the Xth MAS and Bodyguard to BORGHESE.

A. Circumstances of Interrogation:

1. Subject had been arrested in MILAN by persons unknown and placed in the military jail of MILAN. He was identified by IV CIC during a routine check and transferred to the SAN VITTORE jail on 20 June, where he was placed at the disposition of this unit.

B. Personal Details:

2. Name: BORDOGNA, Mario
   Born: 4/5/20 at MILAN
   Father: fu Carlo
   Mother: TEVAROTTO, Elvira
   Residence: Via VANBITELLI, 41, MILAN

C. Military Service:

3. Subject volunteered as a parachutist in the last months of 1941. After training he was sent to the officers candidate school at BRA, being graduated in June 1943

4. Subject was sent to TARQUINIA as an instructor. On 2nd September he fled in search of a unit still intact, and to avoid being sent to a concentration camp by the Germans. In MANTOVA, where Subject had gone to hide with a girlfriend, he learned of the existence of a unit in TRIESTE and left to join it.

D. Contact with the Xth MAS:
5. In TRIESTE Subject learned that the unit did not exist. He met Commandante BARDELLI, whom he had known at the parachute school, and who offered him a position in the Xth MAS which was at that time still in the process of formation.
6. Subject accepted and with BARDELLI went to POLA for supplies which were taken to LA SPEZIA.

E. BARBARIGO Battalion:
7. In LA SPEZIA, BARDELLI was forming the BARBARIGO Battalion. Suject, as his aide, was given command of the First Company. With the battalion he saw action in several engagements on the NETTUNO front. During the Easter day (1944) inspection he was introduced to BORGHESE.
8. After the tour of duty at the front, Subject accompanied BARDELLI to IVREA and LA SPEZIA as BARDELLI was entrusted by the General Staff of the Xth MAS with the task of forming a regiment with the BARBARIGO. LUPO and SAGITTARIO Battalions.
9. This reorganisation was still under way when BARDELLI was killed by the Partisans at ORZENGO on 8 July 1944.

F. Subject becomes BORGHESE's Bodyguard:
10. At BARDELLI's funeral, Subject again met BORGHESE who asked him to become one of his aides. Subject accepted this offer and went with BORGHESE to LONATO where the General Headquarters of the Xth MAS was located to
11. BORDOGNA's specific assignment was to act as BORGHESE's bodyguard. Although he accompanied BORGHESE everywhere he never took part in any discussions nor performed any administrative or other work for him. He states that he accompanied

BORGHESE on a number of occasions when the latter had meetings with WOLF, RAHN and HARSTER [referred to below].

12. Subject was asked about his relations with BUTTAZONI [Captain in X MAS]. States that he knew him at the parachute school. He had no other contacts with BUTTAZONI and denies knowing of his activities with the GIS [German Intelligence Service].

G. Comments

13. Subject is a confirmed Fascist who states that he believed in the Fascist cause and is still of the same opinion. He maintains that if necessary he will still fight the Allies.

14. He denies any connection with either sabotage or espionage organisations.

15. Subject has spoken freely and it is believed he has told the truth.

16. The files of this unit and those of SCI 3 have been checked for traces on Subject with negative results.

H. Recommendations:

17. It is recommended that BORDOGNA be interned as dangerous to the Allied cause unless it is believed that he should be interrogated by CSDIC in reference to the movements and activities of Prince Valerio BORGHESE. Interrogation conducted and report written by SCI Unit Z, MILAN. (Ibid.)

SS Obergruppenfuhrer Karl Wolff, the Supreme SS and Police leader in Italy was described by an American wartime journalist.

Among the wealthiest and most exquisite of the SS plunderers was Gen. Karl Wolff, supreme commander of the *Waffen* or fighting SS, and police chief of Nazi-held Italy. An explosive, hard, blond Aryan, General Wolff had been a

116

personal adjutant to Himmler. Coming to Italy of a high post at Fuhrer headquarters. (Davis, Forrest, 'The Secret History of a Surrender,' *Saturday Evening Post*, 22 September 1945)

Rudolph Rahn was the German Plenipotentiary to Mussolini's Italian Social Republic. General Wilhelm Harster was the head of the German security police and Sicherheitsdienst in Italy. All were reported to have been involved in the rounding up and deportation of an estimated 8,000 Jews to concentration camps.

On 11 July 1945, 38 Field Security Section sent a request to CS Centre Bari to arrest Umberto Luciani. He had been identified as a stay-behind radio operator of the X Flotilla Mas who had left Bologna on 23 or 24 April to visit his family at Torino di Sangro. When arrested they were to inform Captain Roberts at Headquarters No. 3 District. Luciani was located and arrested by 808 Battalion on 29 July and held at a local prison where he was questioned.

The next document was a report of Giovanni Tausani, another captured radio operator, dated 25 July. He had been questioned by a CSDIC officer.

CSDIC/"I"/Zi 974 SECRET
25 July 1945
Attachments no. 2
QUESTIONED:
No. 850: Chief of the 1st class TAUSANI Giovanni – son of Ernesto and late Sabina CAUSER – Born in TRIESTE on 12.6.1905 – address: MONTORFANO (Como Province) Via Brianza No. 7.
PREAMBLE: Chief of the 1st class R.T.[Radio/Wireless Telegraphy] - on 8 September '43 he was with the "N.P." [???] Group of LIVORNO. Finding himself without means of subsistence he enlisted in the Special Groups of the "VEGA" Bn. for radio links of the MILANO Group. (see re;877/Zi) Currently detained in the prison of "S.DONINO", COMO.
JUDGMENT OF THE INTERROGATION OFFICER:
A serious person, precise in his explanations. He seems honest, but he appears dejected both for the arrest and for the concern for his family. The person being questioned is a radio operator and a technician and has 25 years of experience in

the radio field. He seems to be a morally honest person, a victim more than anything of circumstances and bad luck. He would be willing to take up the acquittal service to intercept any calls from other members of the "VEGA" network.

HISTORY:

8.9.43 - He served with the "N.P." Group in LIVORNO.

10.9.43 – He leaves the unit which had already been disbanded.

10.10.43 – He meets Captain BUTTAZZONI in LA SPEZIA. He is enlisted in the X Mas and assigned to secretarial work.

12.12.43 – He is transferred to IESOLO with the battalion.

1.5.44 – He is transferred to MONTORFANO, Head of Post R.T.

1.3.45 – He hears about the dissolution of the "VEGA" Bn. and its transformation into "S" Groups.

12.4.45 – Finally, 2nd Head BALDO Reno goes to Piazza Squadrismo 10, to Mare GHERARDELLI, owner of a radio repair shop.

14.4.45 – He connects with Sergeant VILLA Sergio of the "CECCACCI" Group (TREVISO). He also connects with 2nd Head CAMI Alessandro of the "GENOA" Group. He is unable to connect with Head LUCIANI of the "CUCCHIARA" Group (MODENA).

From 14 to 24.4.45 - He makes a daily connection with the "CECCACCI" Group.

4/25/45 – Destroys the transmitting equipment.

4/28/45 – Goes to COMO with his family.

5/8/45 – Reports himself, as ordered by the C.L.N. announcement, to the "DE CRISTOPHORIS" Barracks. He is held under arrest on the complaint of the S. Capo [Chief] D'ANNIBALI Ezio, who had already been part of the "SS" of VERONA.

5/15/45 – Transferred to the "XXV April" Barracks – COMO.

5/30/45 – Transferred to the "S. DONINO" prison – COMO.

REPORTS ON:

Radiotelegraphers of the Connection Network – V Column "VEGA" Bn.

Apr. 45 – Group of "MILANO" (VENUTA) Capo   R.T. TAUSANI Giovanni

Maro[?seaman]

GHIRARDELLI Gino

Group of "TREVISO" (CECCACCI) Sergeant R.T. VILLA Sergio

Group of "TREVISO" (CUCCHIARA) Chief of R.T. of 3 LUCIANI Umberto

Group of "GENOVA" (LINETTI) 2nd Chief of R.T. CAMI Alessandro, who is perhaps still at liberty.

- Ciphers used: (see attached diagram).
- Equipment: Each Group has noted a receiving and transmitting device of the following type:

  - Power: 20 Watts
  - Transmitter 6 C 5 pilot
  - PE 0640 amplifier
  - Receiver: 6-valve superheterodyne
  - Power supply with rectifier valve:
    5 x 4
    Manufacturer: FERRI Company of COMO
    Closed in a suitcase weighing approximately 25 Kg.

Daily appointments:

10 am - Excluding Sundays - on wave 5600 Khz.

The questioned does not believe that the network still works, but he declares himself willing to provide a listening service to intercept or call the other Groups.

Scheme of the ciphers used by the "VEGA" Bn special groups.

For communications, a mnemonic cipher code studied by the Telecommunications office of the X Mas of LONATO should have been used, which I transcribe:

1st Organization: transcription of the alphabet with normal sequence:

A B C D E F G H I J K L M N O P Q R S T U V W X Y Z
7 18 14 8 21 23 9 15 1 19 10 2 25 16 3 11 22 4 20 12 5 17 26 6 13 24

2nd Operation: using a key group, for example 80921, obtain the alphabet with variable sequence:

From the key group 8 – and an arbitrary filler number.

Of the key group 09 – It means that you have to count 9 places on the normal sequence alphabet to get the first letter of the variable sequence alphabet. In the case of e.g. the letter I.

Of the key group 21 _ 2+1 (duo + uno) equals 3.

From the letter I obtained, counting 3 places (excluding the I) on the normal sequence alphabet we get the letter L; so then three more places we get the letter O.

Then write down the variable sequence alphabet:

I L O R U X A D G X P T Y C H N V B J S E U F Z M W

3rd Operation: Key phrase: e.g. "Therefore sit comfortably on the knees of a comely woman."

To encrypt the telegram to "I'M LEAVING TOMORROW" proceed as follows:

1st Write the key phrase above the telegram in clear text:

SEDER MIQUIN

I'M LEAVING TOMORROW

2nd Referring to the variable sequence alphabet obtained in prison, the letter S (first letter of the key phrase) in order from left to right up to the letter P (first letter of the telegram to encrypt).

Doing the operation for all the letters we will obtain the following groups of two digits:

17 12 22 17 25 09 02 03 02 15 11

3rd Collect the groups of numbers in groups of 5 digits each:

17122 21725 09020 30215 11

Since the last group is incomplete, we complete it with 3 arbitrary recapitulating numbers:

17122 21725 09020 30215 11077.

4th Operation: Overencrypt the text obtained in the first cipher using an easily remembered Group: for example 24.5.1935 and write below over the text in the first cipher and perform the subtraction without carrying: Example:

Group of the 2nd cipher written below:

24519	35245	19352	45193	52451

Text in the 1st cipher: 17122 21725 09020 30215 11077

Subtraction without
Carrying: 17497 14520 10332 15988 41484
– Text in the 2nd cipher.

This decides the telegram in the 2nd cipher to be transmitted.

To decipher: perform the reverse operation tends to present, that the numbers obtained must be counted on the alphabet in a sporadic sequence from right to left.

I declare that what is stated corresponds to the pure truth and that I am at my complete disposal for all clarifications regarding the R.T. service as well as facts and people of my knowledge formerly belonging to the former VEGA Bn. Of the X Mas.

COMO 14 July 1945 Chief R.T. 1st Class signed Giovanni TAUSANI.

ATTACHMENT No. 2

Personal report of the questioned no. 850:

I, the undersigned TAUSANI Giovanni son of Ernesto, born in TRIESTE on 12.6.1905, Marshal of the former "VEGA" Bn. of the X Mas of MONTORFANO, states the following: At the beginning of the month of June 44 the "N.P." Bn. [Paratroopers Swimmers of X MAS] that was in IESOLO split up and I was transferred to MONTORFANO together with the R.T. personnel: Serg. MAZZUCCATO Leone, Serg. FANCELLU Giovanni, S.C.R.T. [???], and NARDO Carmine, the latter declassified for inability to receive.

As a Comrade "NP." transferred to MONTECCHIO at the Under-secretariat of the Navy, I was ordered to establish R.T. contacts with said companies. The service was carried out with three daily appointments on 5,600 Khz. Shortly after arriving in MONTORFANO, Sergeant FANCELLU left the unit and was transferred to the disposal of the German Navy. With the transfer of the "VEGA" Bn. to PIEDMONT, I was ordered to get in touch with said Bn. The service was carried out by appointments on the 5,600 Khz band. Both with MONTECCHIO and with the "N.P." Bn. the secret code of the Ministry of the Navy was used, already in use at the "N.P." Bn. before September 8, 1943.

In October 1944 the sergeant MAZZUCCATO Leone was transferred to VERONA at the German "S" [?Security]. The S.C. GREGGIO Giacomo of the "N.P." Bn. of CASASCO was transferred to MONTORFANO.

On November 1, 1944 the "VEGA" Bn. of MONTORFANO was included in the radiotelegraph network of the X Mas. For this service codes, names and ciphers issued by the Communications Office of the S.M. of the Navy of LONATO were used.

Subsequently the following operators were assigned to the "VEGA" Bn. in MONTORFANO: Chief, R.T. LUCIANI Umberto and Serg. Te R.T. VILLA Sergio, coming from the Radio of TURIN, 2nd Chief CAMI Alessandro, coming, I believe, from the X Mas detachment of MILAN and the 2nd Chief BALDO Remo coming from the Radio of MILAN.

At the beginning of March, rumors began to circulate about the dissolution of the "VEGA" Bn.

Towards the middle of that month, Lieutenant CUCCHIARA Elio, the seaman PANCALDI and the Chief LUCIANI left for MODENA or BOLOGNA.

Subsequently, Sergeant VILLA left for TREVISO with the T.V. [???] Group CECCACCI. For GENOA, with the S.T. [???] LINETTI, the 2nd Chief CAMI left. For TURIN, the S.T. MAMBELLI with Sergeant PARI and the S.C. GREGGIO Giacome. The morning after this last departure, returning to the barracks he learned that the truck on the road to TURIN had blown up and the driver and S.C. [???] GREGGIO had died. The radio had not suffered significant damage and the rescue truck delivered it to the station.

On April 2nd, listening on the radio-telegraph network of the X Mas (5450 Khz) he heard Sergeant VILLA of the CECCACCI Group for the first time.

On April 5th at 10 am, from the 2nd Chief BALDO Remo, listening in MONTORFANO, Chief LUCIANI was heard for the first time with signal strength 1 + 2, while LUCIANI was heard from MONTORFANO strength 1.

On April 6th in the afternoon, I was called by Commander T.V. ROSSI who ordered me to collect the archives increasing the R.T. communications. and the following morning with Commander ROSSI, Lieutenant Commander COZZI, S.T. VENUTA, driver CICERI, I was taken to LONATO where I was told to present myself at the Telecommunications Office for the delivery of the archive, which I handed over to the Chief Quartermaster in charge of the aforementioned office. In LONATO I saw T.V. CECCACCI arriving from TREVISO who made the trip with them to the BAITELLA where T. V. ROSSI, Lt. Comm. GOZZI, S.T. VENUTAn and T.V. CECCACCI got off at the Direction of the Commissariat. I arrived in MONTORFANO very late that same evening. On 12 April I was ordered to load the material onto a truck that was ready for departure with other material and food, escorted by Sergeant LANGUI and which was to go to MILAN. Together with me, 2nd Chief BALDO and the following material were loaded: 2 radio suitcases - - 2 SAFAR receivers - 1 power supply for the aforementioned - accumulators and other material - washing tools, which we unloaded in Piazza Squadrismo 12 at GHIRARDELLI who had a workshop for the repair of radio equipment. On April 14 I heard and communicated with Sergeant VILLA and for the first time since his arrival I heard 2nd Chief CAMI, while I could not hear Chief LUCIANI despite repeated calls to him. In the evening, since it was Saturday, I took the train to COMO and went home to my family to spend Sunday, leaving 2nd Chief BALDO for any communications. From MONTORFANO I returned to MILAN on Monday, April 16.

On Wednesday, April 18, I was ordered to report to Via Annunciata where Lieutenant GOZZI had his office, at a mirror and glass company on the 2nd floor, where I found Commander T.V. ROSSI who ordered me to pay attention to communications with GENOA since he was leaving for there and if the trip was good I would have 2nd Chief CAMI repeat the letter "R" three times. Together with me also came the 2nd Chief BALDO who received the order to be ready to leave for TURIN.

On the morning of April 20th, the seaman ZULIAN came to call me and informed me that I had to go to p.za [???Piazza] Cairoli where in a cafe I would find Ten. GOZZI and the S.T. VENUTA. I went to the appointment accompanied by the 2nd Chief BALDO, the Seaman GHIRARDELLI and the Sergeant PARI who from TURIN had come to MILAN to pick up BALDO and reach TURIN together. I communicated to Ten. GOZZI that I had received the three "R"s from the 2nd Chief CAMI. Lt. GOZZI instructed me to inform BALDO to be ready because Sergeant PARI had come from TURIN to accompany them on the trip. I replied that I had

already seen PARI and that BALDO had been notified of
PARI himself.
At the daily appointments at 10 o'clock I could always hear
Sergeant VILLA well, occasionally 2nd Chief CAMI and I was
no longer able to hear Chief LUCIANI, despite repeatedly
calling him.
On Saturday 21 April I took the 8:00 pm train to COMO to
spend Sunday with my family, still leaving 2nd Capo BALDO
in MILAN. Arriving home that evening, I had complaints
from my wife who complained that going a week without
seeing me was too much. She said that there were so many
workers who left in the morning to go and work in MILAN
and returned home that evening. I promised her that I would
come on Wednesday to leave on Thursday morning and on
Saturday to leave on Monday.
Upon my return to MILAN on Monday morning 23 April, I
no longer found 2nd Capo BALDO and from
GHIRARDELLI I learned that he had left together with
PARI, taking the apparatus, trying to reach TURIN. On
Wednesday 25 April, around 11:00, I received a phone call
informing me to show up in the afternoon at Ten.te GOZZI
to pick up some biscuits. Around 16:00 I left the house
together with Mare GHIRARDELLI. We waited in vain for
the tram. After getting information we learned that since
15:00 all the trams had returned to the depot. We decided to
go on foot. As we were walking along the streets, passing in
front of the Northern railway, I noticed that the gates were
closed and no one was stationed nearby. I pointed out to
GHIRARDELLI that my trip to COMO was about to be
ruined. The people passing by on the street were showing
signs of nervousness and everyone was trying to get home
quickly.
I had a clear vision that some exceptional event would happen
during the night. I took the biscuits and in the office of
Lieutenant GOZZI I noticed the S.T. SESSA the Maro
FABBRO and the S.C. BATTINI.
Going back home this impression of mine had to be
confirmed because passing in front of the barracks an unusual

display of force was noted, especially in front of the barracks of the German gendarmerie behind the house where I lived. Returning home and without waiting for orders from anyone, together with GHIRARDELLI we proceeded to demolish the apparatus, demolition completed in the early hours of the following morning. I stayed at home waiting for a half-day to COMO and finally on Sunday 29 April the train service to COMO was restored and I took the 18.45 train. When the announcement of presentation came, I showed up on the first day, that is, May 8th at 3:00 p.m., at the "DE CHRISTOFORIS" Barracks. Having served in the Royal Navy for 23 years, where I was raised at the age of 16, my soul rebelled against committing any crime that was not legal and honest, and without waiting for orders of any kind, I told GHIRADELLI, who was looking at me questioningly, that it was our duty to proceed with the destruction of the equipment. I am convinced that the other operators also did the same, because according to the demands that were revealed to the preceding of the presence of each Group, the personnel were not at all happy with the service that they had to perform, which was known exclusively to the Commander himself. To aggravate this discontent with cars well supplied with money and comforts, while the sailors even skimped on their cigarettes. In the very good period that I spent in MILAN, while the officers had trucks of food and other goods at their disposal, I and GHIRARDELLI ate at the war canteen. At one time we had a royal relief, rather, of 10 packets of biscuits of three biscuits in each packet.

NOTE: The report was sent by the Center "E" - A copy has already been distributed on 18.7.45:
- to the A.C of S.G.2 (C.I.) AFHQ - MILAN
- to the GAS.I. - 2 District -   MILAN
- to the S.C.I ....MILAN
- to the S.C.I/Z................................MILAN
- to the Centre C.S. ....MILAN (Ibid.)

August 1945

On 7 August, Colonel Earle B. Nichols, G.S.C, the Assistant to the Acting Chief of Staff, G-2, sent the following note to the Commandant at the Combined Mediterranean Forces (CMF)' "R" Camp.

SUBJECT: FRASSONI Alessandro
             ARDITO Stefano
Reference the above named who are understood to be both interned in your camp.
These two were originally recommended for release by the agency interrogating them. 15 AG [Army group] letter 1402/24/GSI(b) dated 1 July 1945 to this HQ draws attention to this recommendation but states that both subjects had already been evacuated to TERNI.
In view of their youth (their ages are stated to be 15 and 18 respectively),(and the fact that the evidence against them is not unduly strong, it is suggested that their cases be made the subject of an early review by the Board with a view to release to which this section will not raise any objection.(Ibid.)

Over the following weeks there were reports that Cucchiari, Cennacci, Rizzoli and Bonaccini had been arrested.
On 27 August, DISTHREE, the codename for a military wireless operator, sent FREEDOM, the codename for the operator at G-2 CI Section the following telegram:

GI 815 SECRET, Arrest reported DI CARLUCCIO Aniello di Eduardo. Arrested by 808 Bn CS NAPLES on 25. Described as enemy agent ex GAMMA Group 10 Flot MAS. CS interrogation proceeding. (Ibid.)

Luciani's interrogation was not submitted until 30 August.

REPORT ON THE DETAILED INTERROGATION OF AGENT LUCIANI UMBERTO.
1) GENERAL INFORMATION

House and name: LUCIANO Umberto
Alias N.N.
Date and place of birth: 15.11.1903 in Torino di Sangro
(Chieti)
Nationality: Italian
Name and address of close relatives:
Father: Nicola son of Giovanni, aged 67, retired from the
FF.SS. [???], living in the seaside village of Torino di Sangro;
Mother: BIANCHI Marianna son of Luigi, 65 years old,
housewife, living in the Marina district of Torino di Sangro'
Wife: AMICUCCI Giccondina son of Giacinto and Rossi
Maria, born on 19/5/1913 in Palmoli (Chieti), postal receiver
in Torino di Sangro
Children: Nicola, born on 21 March 1936 in Torino di Sangro:
Concezio, born on 1/1/1938 in Torino di Sangro.
Domicile: Torino di Sangro – via Fiorello La Guardia
Profession: Postal Substitute
Features: height 1.67m; straight brown hair; brown eyes;
brown color; oval face, robust build; shaved beard; regular
forehead; special features N.N.
Known languages: a few elements of French.

2) CHRONOLOGY
After attending the first nautical institute, on 12/2/1923 he
was called up for military service, and assigned to the
C.R.E.M. [???] of Pola, from where he was transferred to
Varignano (La Spezia) to attend a radio-telegraphist course.
In November of that year he was assigned to the R/T station
De la Maddalena and on 1/12/1924 he was promoted to sub-
chief.
De La Maddalena reached La Spezia and was embarked on
the submarine "Pietro Micca", remaining there until June
1926, when he was assigned to the r.t. station of Arma di
Taggia (San Remo).
On 1 December 1927 he was sent on leave to Torino di
Sangro, where he remained inactive until 1931, when he found
employment at the company deme [illegible] Sangritana" in
Bomba.
Following the bankruptcy of that company he remained
unemployed for some time and in 1934 he obtained the post

of collector at the Municipal Tax Office of Perano (Chieti), for which he worked until 1935.

In March 1935 he was recalled to arms, but not being declared fit for the A.O. as he suffered from chronic malaria, he was sent home.

The following September he was again recalled and assigned to the battalion of S. Marco in Pola, with which he first reached Taranto and on 1 April 1936 Massawa. From there he went to Addis Ababa and in February 1937 he returned to Pola, from where on the 28th of that month he was sent back on leave.

He returned to Torino di Sangro and performed the duties of a postal substitute until 7 April 1939, when he was recalled and embarked on the cruiser "Fiume" as second chief.

After an 80-day period of convalescence leave, for exudative pleurisy, he resumed embarking on the aforementioned cruiser, from which on 31 October 1939 he was invited back on leave, due to supervening physical disability, a consequence of the pleurisy.

On 16/6/1940, once again recalled, he was sent to Venice and embarked on the flagship "California", following the sinking of which he was transferred to the C.R.E.M. depot in Brindisi at his disposal.

On 20/11/1941 he joined the C.R.E.M. of Messina and subsequently assigned to the naval communications center of that city where he remained until 14/2/1942, because assigned to San Giorgio Jonico, under the command of the Taranto Marine Communications Center.

On 1 September 1942 he was promoted to third class r.t. chief and in November of the same year assigned to the R/T station of Corfu.

Here he was surprised by the events of 8 September 1943 and after the order to surrender, on the 25th of that month he was taken prisoner by the Germans and interned in a concentration camp in Corfu, then in another camp in Tsamouria.

In January 1944, since he was ordered to go armed to defend himself against rebel attacks while he was cleaning the stables, he pointed out that if he had to take up arms again, this could only happen in his homeland.

Therefore, in the following May he was assigned to Italy for service in the Republican Navy.

Escorted by a German sergeant, he reaches Neubrandenburg; he is accompanied by a German marshal, Bordeaux, where he is hired by the Republican Navy command, after signing the oath form to the RSI.

The subject agrees to serve, because he hopes to be able to join his family.

He is assigned to Chiavari, under the command of frigate captain VAGLIASINTI, then to Casal Monferrato, still under the command of the same officer, to attend a course at the constituent school of marine riflemen and artillerymen; a course that is not carried out for reasons unknown.

He then passes, ex officio, on 1 August 1944, to the assault means report, to the command of corvette captain DI GIACOMO.

He does not remember the names of other elements of the aforementioned unit.

3. FIRST CONTACT WITH THE ENEMY ORGANIZATION

The subject declares that he has never had contact with the German intelligence service.

4. TRAINING

The subject claims that he has never attended any course in espionage and sabotage.

He declares instead that at the beginning of August 1944 he was sent from La Spezia to Arona (Lake Maggiore) at the "SCIRE" battalion – where all the R/T soldiers of the Republican Navy flocked – to attend a training course as a radio operator lasting about three months, at the end of which – 1 November 1944 – he was transferred to the R/T station of the Monte Grappa barracks in Turin, as a radio operator, under the command of frigate captain LISI.

Of the soldiers belonging to the Scire battalion he remembers the commander, corvette captain DI GIACOMO and the sub-lieutenant PACE.

On 27 November 1944, still as a radio operator, and assigned to the "VEGA" battalion, stationed in Montorfano (Como), commanded by Lieutenant ROSSI Mario.

5. FINAL INSTRUCTIONS AND MISSION

The subject declares that he has never carried out any espionage or sabotage mission for the German service.

He states, instead, that he was sent to Bologna, on 27 March 1945, in civilian clothes, by Lieutenant ROSSI Mario, to set up a radio station and connect with the Montorfano command while waiting for orders; but he ignores the reasons for the establishment of this service.

In his company were the paratrooper lieutenant CUCCHIARA Elio, the sub-lieutenant BONACCINI, the sailors RIZZOLI, CENACCHI, PANCALDI, all in civilian clothes, but he does not know what their goals were.

He also does not know whether the group, under the command of Lieutenant CUCCHIARA, had weapons and whether the officer himself had financial availability.

He does not exclude, however, that CUCCHIARA could have been holding funds received from the Montorfano command.

In Bologna, where he arrived on March 29, the subject initially took temporary lodgings in the home of sailor PANCALDI, in a street he does not remember; and after a few days in via Belvedere No. 13 with a certain Mrs. Jole, in a room provided for him by PANCALDI himself, who introduced him as an engineer.

To justify his civilian status, the subject had the municipality of Bologna issue him an identity card with the qualification of employee.

Lieutenant CUCCHIARA and the others, since they were local, went to live in their respective homes, located in an address he is unable to specify.

The radio set is placed in the home of Lieutenant CUCCHIARA's mother (he does not remember the street), who was absent at that time because she was crowded in Bologna itself.

The subject finally asserts that no one in his group, during their stay in Bologna, carries out any activity.

He covers the daily expenses of food with the salary of the month of April of about 8,500 lire received in advance from the commanding officer; the other companions do the same. His accommodation, however, is paid for by Lieutenant CUCCHIARA.

6. DEPARTMENT FOR WHICH THE AGENT WAS TO COMPLETE THE MISSION

The subject specifies once again that he does not know the reasons for his transfer to Bologna and adds that no specific mission had been entrusted to him.

Before leaving Montorfano he had received the order from Lieutenant ROSSI Mario to connect with the command of that location and to await instructions.

7. TRAVEL AND ACTIVITIES UP TO THE TIME OF THE ARREST

The subject declares that he has not made any travel in liberated territory during the time he served for the RSI.

8. NAMES AND ADDRESSES OF OTHER AGENTS

The subject is unable to name any other persons other than those already specified.

9. ACTIVITIES INSPIRED BY THE GERMAN SERVICE TO BE CARRIED OUT AFTER THE SURRENDER

The subject is not aware of any activities inspired by the German service to be carried out after the surrender.

10.) MEANS OF CONNECTION

The subject uses a "Ferri" radio transmitter and receiver to correspond with his command in Montorfano, with which he only connects on 13 April 1945, without transmitting messages using the 55-56 metre long band of the international code

Call sign: LCN; corresponding station call sign: TSN.

The above acronyms were altered using letters of the alphabet, in relation to the day of transmission.

Italian radio set from Second World War
(https://it.topwar.ru/152860-proizvodstvo-otechestvennyh-
sredstv-voennoj-svjazi-v-1940-1945-godah-okonchanie.html)

11.) <u>OBJECTS BELONGING TO THE AGENT</u>
- identity card No. 61035 issued by the municipality of
Bologna on 3 April 1945;
- identity card No. 160158 issued by the municipality of
Torino di Sangro on 3 July 1945;
- A special 20+4 day license ticket issued by the Taranto Navy
Depot Command on 26 July 1945;
- a certificate issued by the Taranto C.R.E.M. Depot –
interrogation office – on 20 July 1945;
- passport-sized photograph of the subject;
- 4 pieces of paper with various notes;
- a military slip for the train journey from Torino di Sangro to
Taranto;
- a ticket for the journey by truck from Chieti to Bologna;

12.) <u>OTHER DETAILS OF SPECIAL INTEREST</u>
Five days before the liberation of Bologna, the subject
received an order from lieutenant CUCCHIARA to destroy
the radio set, an order he carries out using sailor RIZZOLI.

He then occasionally meets under the portico of the Pavaglione with the members of the group and waits for the liberation of the city to go home, having been given permission by commander ROSSI, before undertaking the journey from Montorfano.

The day after the Allies entered Bologna, he learns from sailor RIZZOLI that an English officer is looking for tenant CUCCHIARA and probably also for the subject, who, at the first favorable opportunity – 19 April – through the Red Cross, takes a seat in an Allied car and reaches his family in Torino di Sangro on 6 May.

At the native pass he remained until July 3, on which date he took a bus to Bologna to find out the outcome of the Allied police searches.

Having learned from RIZZOLI's mother that her son and his other companions had been arrested, he continued after about two hours on the same bus to Milan to avoid possible arrest and returned to his family on the morning of July 9, always with the same bus.

On July 16 he went to Taranto and presented himself to the navy depot command to regularize his military position.

He then returned to Torino di Sangro on July 28, 1945 and was arrested.

13.) COMMENTS FROM THE INTERROGATORS

The subject, although clever and intelligent, although he tries to show off calm and at ease, is deliberately reticent and insists on not providing information, especially regarding the last mission in Bologna, appearing particularly surprised when he is told that the units in which he served during the Republican period were engaged in information and sabotage.

It is therefore proposed to consult the competent Allied bodies to find out what evidence they have against LUCIANI, also in relation to the results of the interrogations of Lieutenant CUCCHIARA and members of his group, who have already been arrested.

14.) PLACE OF DETENTION AND PROPOSALS FOR MEASURES TO BE TAKEN

The subject is detained in the judicial prison of Chieti.

No proposal for measures is formulated against him for the reasons set out in no. 13.
Chieti, 30 August 1945

Umberto Luciani's identity cards for Bologna and Torino di Sangro (TNA WO204/12453)

The following day, Major Riccardo Valenti of the Royal Carabinieri in Rome provided additional detail about Luciani and other stay-behind X MAS personnel:

SEEN: the case of LUCIANO Umberto is inseparable from that of his accomplices CUCCHARIA, BONACCINI, RIZZOLI and CENACCHI, already arrested. It is also necessary to examine the statements of the latter for the indispensable objections - possibly integrated by comparisons - to LUCIANI, who appeared reticent. At the present time it is not, therefore, possible to assess the responsibilities of the subject, nor, therefore, to forward proposals.

Appendix A

VAGLIASSINTI – frigate captain, around 44 years old, tall brown, northern commander of the Marina barracks of Chiavari and of the artillery and marine rifleman school of Casalmonfano. Last seen towards the end of July 1944 at Casa Ferrato.

DI GIACOMO – Lieutenant Commander, around 40 years old, tall, gray hair, Tuscan. Commander of the underwater assault vehicle department of the X flotilla mas of La Spezia and therefore of the Scire battalion of Arona. Last seen towards the end of October 1944 in Arona.

LISI – frigate captain, short, former lieutenant colonel of the CC.rsi not better indicated. Commander of the Monte Grappa barracks in Turin. Last seen in Turin on 11/25/1944.

PACE – Second lieutenant of the vessel, short, not better indicated. Officer of the Scire battalion. Last seen towards the end of October 1944 in Arona.

ROSSI Mario – Lieutenant, around 40 years old, dark-haired, tall, northern. Commander of the Vega battalion in Montorfano (Como). Last seen in Montorfano on 27 March 1945.

CUCCHIARA Elio – parachutist lieutenant, around 40 years old, dark-haired, short, from Emilia. Commander of a group of the Republican navy in civilian dress operating in Bologna. Last seen on 21 April 1945 in Bologna. He is currently believed to be in a concentration camp in Modena.

BONACCINI – second lieutenant, 23-24 years old, dark-haired, medium height, from Modena. Element of the CUCCHIARA group, last seen in Bologna in April 1945. He is currently believed to be in a concentration camp in Modena. RIZZOLI – sailor, around 22 years old, dark-haired, tall, from Bologna. Element of the CUCCHIARA group. Last seen in Bologna on 29 April 1945. He is currently believed to be in a concentration camp in Modena. CENACCHI - sailor, tall, dark-haired, 22-23 years old, from Bologna. Element of the CUCCHIARA group. Last seen in Bologna in April 1945. He is currently believed to be in a concentration camp in Modena. PANCALDI – sailor, 27 years old, medium height, blonde, from Bologna. Element of the CUCCHIARA group. Last seen in Bologna in April 1945. He is currently believed to be in a concentration camp in Modena. (Ibid.)

September 1945

On 3 September, Major Camillo Pecorella of the CC.RR. [???] headquarters, submitted the following report on Luciani. Its translation reads:

```
                                              Napoli,  3  settembre    191 5 |10

ISTERO DELLA GUERRA                    Al Comando 3° District

Stato Maggiore R. Esercito
   UFFICIO I. - Sez. 2ª                              N A P O L I
   Centro C. S. di Napoli

N.  9915       di prot.
Risposta al N.
del               Allegati
OGGETTO:      LUCIANI   Umberto.
```

"As a result of sheet no.3/GSI of the 1st andante, the following from the C.S. Center is transcribed for Rome.

As a result of the sheet above, 2 copies of the report on the interrogation to which the well-known LUCIANI Umberto was subjected and the documents seized from him and described in the aforementioned interrogation are transmitted.

In this regard, it should be noted that the person being questioned is precisely the person of interest to the 3rd District.

Since it is not possible, on the basis of the declarations, considered reticent, of LUCIANI Umberto, to propose the adoption of measures against him, and it appears necessary that he be confronted with CUCCHIARA, BONACCINI, RIZZOLI and CENACCHI, already arrested, it is proposed that LUCIANI must be immediately transferred to Naples at the disposal of the Allied body which is interested in the aforementioned accomplices.

We are therefore waiting to know, as quickly as possible - given that we are dealing with a person in a state of detention since 29 July - the decisions of the 3rd District."

There was a note written at the end of September by an officer in the Italian Army's General Staff. Its Google translation reads:

MINISTRY OF WAR RESERVED
ROYAL ARMY GENERAL STAFF P.M. 3800, 26
September 1945

Information Office

N. 101687/2 p.m. of prot.

SUBJECT: NAVY ELEMENTS FORMERLY OF THE "GAMMA" GROUP and the X MAS REPUBLICANS

TO THE GENERAL STAFF OF THE ROYAL NAVY

Department 3 ROME

For information, it is communicated that the Allied Navy Command of VENICE has hired, for its Experimental Center in that city, the following military personnel formerly in service with the X MAS and the "GAMMA" group:

-Ten., Vasc. WOLK	x Eugenio, former Commander of the Gamma group
- Ten. C.N.	x TADINI or Camillo
Lt. Med. MOSCATELLI	x Elvio
S. Lt. WOLNER	x Roberto
Sgt. x FREGUGLIA	o Carlo
Id. x BERNI	o Berno
Id. x NERIGHI	
2 Nocch. x CASTELLI	x Elio
Sgt. x WOLNER	x Enrico
Id x FAEDO	x Amerigo
Id. x SPERBERG	x Rodolfo
Id. x SCARPA	x Mario
Corporal x MONTECCHINI x Ercole	
Sub-command x CAGNOLETTI x Domenico	
- Id. x BIANCHINI	x Domenico
- A.U. x PAMPELLI	x Vito
- A.U. PITACCO	Antonio

All the above-mentioned – as per communication made by the 47 F.S.S. of the place to that C.S. Center – are to be considered discriminated against and immune from any responsibility for the activity carried out by them up to now.

COLONEL CHIEF UDDICIO

E. To Pompeo AGRIFOGLIO (Ibid.)

Written in pencil at the bottom of the page sometime after it had been received was an explanatory note:

X before name = authority for continued employment by RN given by 15 AG letter 1402/1-/QSI(G) of 19 Jun 704-F-2 at 16(c)

x after name = now in Venice

o after name – now in Lu 8.A [sic] XIII Corps letter 59/10/1(G) of 5 Nov 45. (Ibid.)

October 1945

In early October, Giuseppe Pisano, the Commanding Officer of the Counter Sabotage Centre in Cagliari recruited Filippo Lacava, an experienced X MAS officer with pro-Allied sympathies for possible work. His interrogation report was included in the liquidation file.

INTERROGATION REPORT on LACAVA Filippo
1. PERSONAL DETAILS.

Name	LACAVA Filippo
Cover name	-
Born	CAGLIARI, 27 August 1916
Nationality	Italian
Father	Aurelio, died Cagliari, 11 Oct 32.
Mother	Caterina nee MAZZONI, age 55
Brothers	Isidoro, age 22, P.W. in Egypt
	Otello, age 20, student
	Nello, age 16 student
	Paolo, age 13 student
Sisters	Angela, age 34
	Anna, age 31
	Nunzia, age 28
	Maria, age 24, student
	Fedora, age 21
	Aurelia, age 14
Address	n.6 Via Romagna, CAGLIARI,
c/o Margherita SORA	
Profession	Sailor
Description	1.66m. tall – black hair – dark eyes – oval face – dark complexion – thin – clean – shaven.
Photographs	4 attached, 2 front, 2 profile

2. RECRUITMENT BY G.I.S.
    Nil

3. SPECIAL TRAINING IN ESPIONAGE, SABOTAGE AND SECRET COMMUNICATIONS

From Oct.44 to Apr. 45, Subject took part in VALDAGNO in submarine training (in pool) at the unit commanded by Lieut. WOLK Eugenio – Gamma Group of the X MAS Division - without however completing his course training which was to have concluded in VENICE.

4. MISSIONS CARRIED OUT

Nil

5. EMPLOYING AGENCY

X MAS Div. – Gamma saboteurs – Unit commanded by Lieut. WOLK, in VALDAGNO.

6. ANY KNOWLEDGE OF POST-SURRENDER ACTIVITY SPONSORED BY G.I.S.

Nil.

7. DATE AND PLACE OF ARREST.

3 October 1945 – CAGLIARI

8. MOTIVE FOR ACCEPTING RECRUITMENT/MISSION.

Subject was discharged from the army by the "21st Comando Deposito Misto Provinciale" as he refused to join anti-partisan units.

Subject then contacted 2nd Capo GLIEMO Angelo, who was then serving at the "Arsenale Marittimo" of VENICE, but also was a member of the "Martiri del Piave" Partisan Brigade in VENICE, commanded by Lt. Col. Franco DE ANTONI.

GLIEMO, who is at present a municipal employee in the Commune of MILAN, advised subject to enrol in the Gamma Group of the X MAS Div. , where he would never have been called upon to operate actively in favour of the Germans or the fascists.

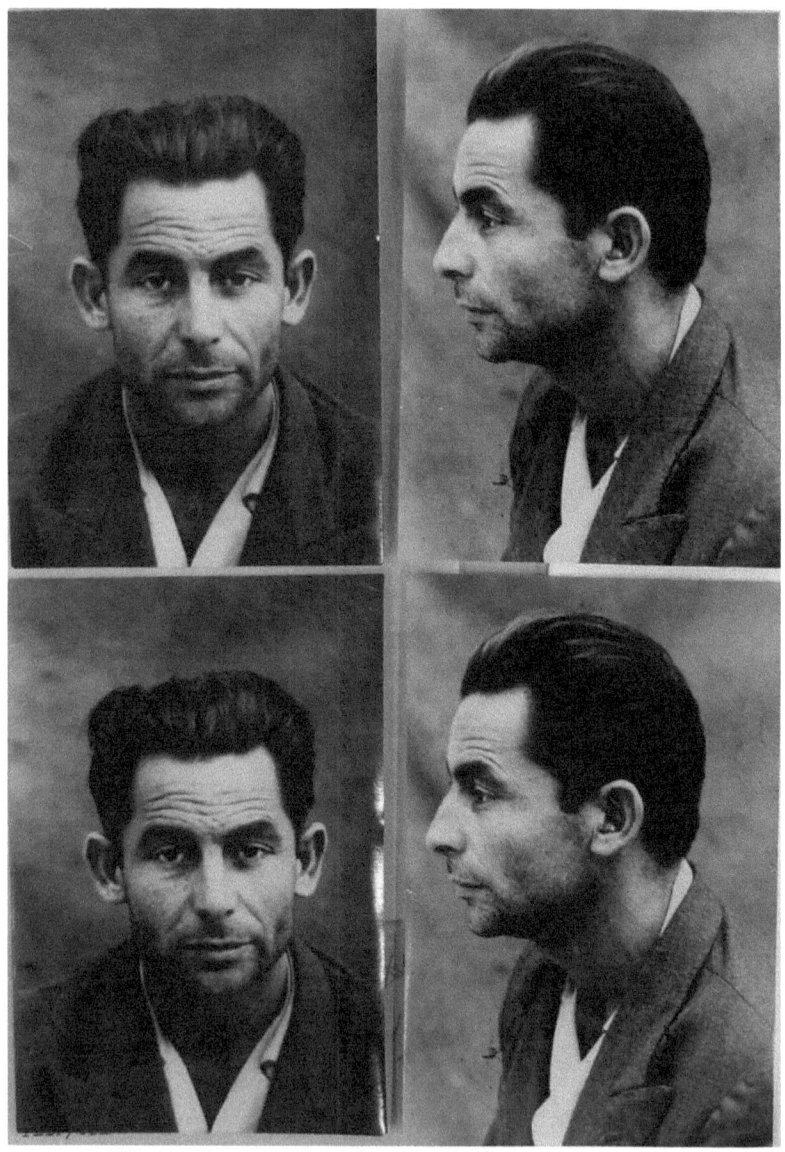

Filippo Lacava (TNA WO204/12452, 6 October 1945)

Exactly what assistance Lacava provided the Allies was not specified.

Captain James Angleton, the Commanding Officer of the SCI/Z Units, sent a copy of the Italian Army's letter with the following note to Colonel Nichols on 16 October. It was marked for his eyes only.

Subject: Immunity granted to former X MAS personnel

1. Through our agent JK 1/8 we received the attached communication addressed by Colonel Pompeo AGRIFOGLIO to the Royal Italian Navy. In this communication AGRIFOLIO states on Allied authority. namely a letter from 47 F.S.S., that a specific group of former X MAS personnel of the "GAMMA" group being used by an Allied Experimental Station in Venice. He concludes by stating that these individuals, on the basis of the 47 F.S.S. Letter R to be considered discriminated and immune from whatever charges or activity conducted heretofore.

2. This office checked with commander HORAN of ONI [Office of Naval Intelligence – US] who stated that his command would not deal with ex-Fascists kept on a purely POW footing. He is unaware of any American Navy authority who has agreed to granting blanket immunity to X MAS personnel.

3. It will be noted that among these 18 "GAMMA" personalities figure such personalities as:
a) S.Ten. Roberto WOLNER, Who carried on clandestine underwater operations against the Allies;
b) Ten. Vasc. Eugenio WOLK, Who was the outstanding figure in "GAMMA" operations and who personally developed secret weapons for naval sabotage. An unconfirmed rumor states that WOLK and one or two friends had planned prior to the Armistice to sell secret weapons developed by the "GAMMA". WOLK what is considered pro-Russian and anti-Anglo-American In view of his Ukrainian origin. It was maintained at Russia would welcome secret naval weapons as they lacked the means to build a fleet and would have to depend on sabotage weapons manned by suicide volunteers.

c) Ten. G.N. Camillo TADINI took part in the Gibraltar attacks of 1943.

d) Serg. Vittori STRADI has been signalled as having been assigned a post-occupational sabotage role.

4. Many of the others are well known in CI Bulletins and have been signalled as resolute enemies of the Allies. For this reason we would appreciate being reassured of the following:

a) That the above immunity has been granted with the knowledge of your command,

b) That the competent American Naval technicians and authorities are aware of the work and establishment of the Venice Experimental Center, and

c) That these individuals have been thoroughly interrogated as to the development of naval sabotage by the republican Navy, which information has been made accessible to the American Naval Command.

5. This office has no record of any interrogation reports issued on the above-mentioned personalities.

SECRET (CONTROL)

(Col. Earle B. Nichols only) (Ibid, 16 October 1945)

On 22 October an issue was highlighted regarding the rewards which the Counter Intelligence Corps had offered for information leading to the arrest of suspected Fascists and German collaborators.

Major M.A. Tonini, the Supervising Agent at CIC Milan Detachment Zone 3, APO 512 c/o GSI(b) DISTRICT 2-CMF contacted the Chief of CIC, [probably Springarn] AFHQ, APO 512, U.S. Army.

Subject: BERTOZZI, Umberto
Lt. of Ufficio "E", 10th Flotilla MAS.

1. CIC, IV Corp assisted in arrest of subject in the early part of May 1945. Since that date this office has been bothered by people who claim to have assisted in the arrest and therefore claim a right to an alleged reward which was offered for his capture. Although claim is made that he

was wanted as a war criminal in the La Specia [sic] area, no record of a reward can be found there.

2. Request this office be advised if any record of reward exists at AFHQ. (Ibid, 22 October 1945)

Major J.H. Aitken for the GSO.I., Allied Screening Commission, replied stating that 'The matter does not concern this Commission, and we have no information on which to base an observation.' The matter did not rest there.

On 29 October, Colonel Nichols sent the following note to SSO (Sy) Med. and COMNAVNOR, US Navy NAPLES, for the attention of the Security Officer. A copy was also sent to SCI Unit 'Z' in Rome.

Subject 10 Flotilla MAS

It is understood that certain members of 10 Flotilla MAS "Gamma" Group , as per attached list, are being, or were, at one time employed by Allied Naval authorities in Venice after the collapse of the German forces in Italy.

It is also understood that five of the a/m [above mentioned] personnel, namely TADINI Camillo, MERIGHI (MERAGHI), Guilio, MONTI Franco, FREGUGLIA (FRAGGALI) Carlo and BERNI Berno were applied for for service in the USA (letter AS-2 of 30 Jun 45 from COMUSNAPNAW to C.I.C. Med., copies to PMG [?Provisional Military Government] MTOUSA [Mediterranean Theatre of Operations USA] GI, MTOUSA and G2 MTOUSA, refers).

It would be appreciated if this Section could be informed as to the present interest the Allied Naval authorities may have in these men in order that their status may be clarified since, at the termination of their special employment, it is felt that they should normally be processed as PW/SEP [Specially employed person]. (Ibid.)

On the same day Nichols contacted GSI Main HQ XIII Corps, CMF attaching three pages of information about the men in the "Gamma" Group.

Subject: 10 Flotilla MAS

Information is required as to the present status of the members of 10 Flotilla MAS is named in the attached list. Please confirm (a) that they have been located; (b) that they are still subject to special employment; (c) that if such special employment is now terminated they have been disposed of as PW/SEP, being members of the Republican Fascist armed forces (This HQ letter of 9 Oct 45 subject and reference as above, also refers).

It is noted that so far only WOLK, SCARPA and SPERBER appear to have been interrogated, very briefly, from the CI standpoint. (Ibid.)

SECRE1

WOLK, Eugenio
(1) Arrest notified by 15 AG, CIS Staff Bulletin 1403/7/CSI (b) of 14 Jun 45

(2) Interrogation report forwarded by 15 AG letter ref 1455/2/GSI (b) of 29 Jun 45 which letter states that WOLK is to be further interrogated (no further interrogation report, however, received).

(3) SSO (Sy) letter 283/211 of 14 Jul 45 states that WOLK is believed to be employed by the Allies.

(4) 15 AG CI B Ser 57 of 7 Jan 45 No. 34.

TADINI, Carmillo
(1) Mentioned in nominal roll prepared by 47 PSS (ref SEC/21/1 of 21 Jun 45) of 10 Flotilla MAS personnel employed on special duties which was forwarded by 15 AG letter 1402/10/GSI (b) of 29 Jun 45

(2) Applied for by COMUSNFNWAW letter to CIC Mediterranean ref A8-2 of 30 Jun 45.

(3) AAI CI B Ser 38 of 9 Dec 44 No. 21.

MOSCATELLI, Elvio
Subject of interrogation report by CSDIC/"I", ref CSDIC/"I"/Z1 812.

WOLNER, Roberto
AFHQ Circular GBI.389.704/1 Ser 37 of 24 Jan 45 No. 139.

FREGUGLIA, Carlo
(1) Name also given as FRAGUGLIA and FRAGGALI.

(2) Mentioned in nominal roll prepared by 47 PSS (ref SEC/21/1 of 21 Jun 45) of 10 Flotilla MAS personnel employed in special duties forwarded by 15 AG letter 1402/10/GSI (b) of 29 Jun 45.

(3) Applied for by COMUSNFNWAW letter ref A8-2 of 30 Jun 45 to CIC Med.

(4) Mentioned in Appendix to a/m report on WOLK as being employed by Royal Navy.

- 1 -
SECRE1

146

RNI, Berno   (1) Name also given as BERNO Berni

                          (2) Mentioned as under PREGUGLIA (2),(3) & (4).

MERIGHI, Giulio   (1) Name also given as MERAGHI, Julio

                          (2) Mentioned as under PREGUGLIA (2),(3) & (4).

CASTELLI, Elfio   (1) Mentioned as under PREGUGLIA (2) & (4).

                          (2) AFHQ Circular GBI.704/1 Ser 57 of 4 Feb 45
                               No. 226.

WOLNER, Enrico   (1) Name also given as WOLNER

                          (2) Mentioned as under PREGUGLIA (2) & (4).

                          (3) AFHQ Circular GBI.704/1 Ser 37 of 24 Jan 45
                               No. 138.

FAEDO, Amerigo   (1) Name also given as FALDO and forename as
                               Alberico.

                          (2) Mentioned as under PREGUGLIA (2) & (4).

                          (3) AFHQ Circular GBI.389.704/1 Ser 32 of 21
                               Jan 45 No. 104.

MONTECCHINI, Ercole   Mentioned as under PREGUGLIA (2) & (4).

CAGNOLETTI, Domenico (1) Name also given as DELLA CAGNOLETTA.

                      (2) Mentioned as under PREGUGLIA (2) & (4)

BIANCHINI, Domenico   Mentioned as under PREGUGLIA (2) & (4).

TAMPELLI, Vito   (1) Name also given as PAMPELLI

                          (2) Mentioned as under PREGUGLIA (2) & (4).

PITACCO, Antonio

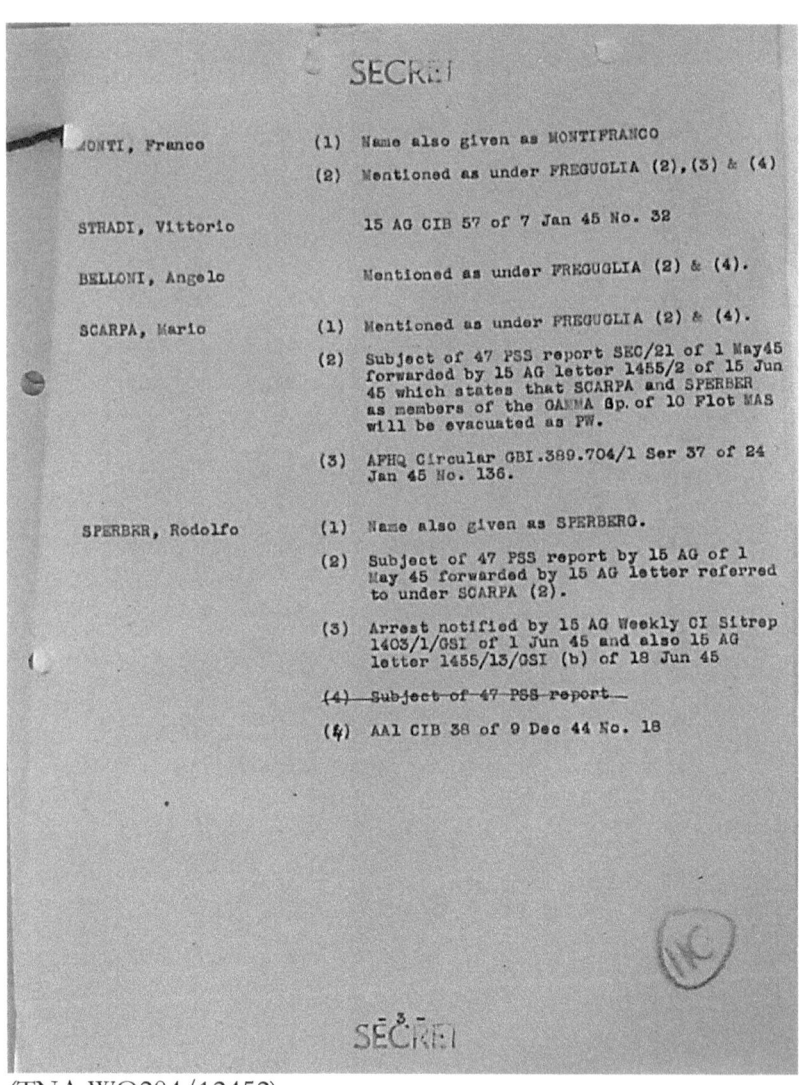

MONTI, Franco   (1)   Name also given as MONTIFRANCO

                      (2)   Mentioned as under FREGUGLIA (2),(3) & (4)

STRADI, Vittorio   15 AG CIB 57 of 7 Jan 45 No. 32

BELLONI, Angelo   Mentioned as under FREGUGLIA (2) & (4).

SCARPA, Mario   (1)   Mentioned as under FREGUGLIA (2) & (4).

                      (2)   Subject of 47 PSS report SEC/21 of 1 May45 forwarded by 15 AG letter 1455/2 of 15 Jun 45 which states that SCARPA and SPERBER as members of the GAMMA Sp. of 10 Flot MAS will be evacuated as PW.

                      (3)   APHQ Circular GBI.389.704/1 Ser 37 of 24 Jan 45 No. 136.

SPERBER, Rodolfo   (1)   Name also given as SPERBERG.

                      (2)   Subject of 47 PSS report by 15 AG of 1 May 45 forwarded by 15 AG letter referred to under SCARPA (2).

                      (3)   Arrest notified by 15 AG Weekly CI Sitrep 1403/1/GSI of 1 Jun 45 and also 15 AG letter 1455/13/GSI (b) of 18 Jun 45

                      (4)   Subject of 47 PSS report

                      (4)   AA1 CIB 38 of 9 Dec 44 No. 18

(TNA WO204/12452)

Carluccio's interrogation report was written towards the end of October by Brigadier Michele Giannatasio of the Naples Counter Sabotage Section. Carluccio claimed to have been born on 18 January 1918 in Naples and gave his occupations as a driver to a fruit dealer.

1. DESCRIPTION

1.72m, slim build, black hair brushed back, shaved beard, light eyes, dark complexion, no moustache. Distinguishing features: 5 teeth surmounted by metal dental plate.

2. RECRUITMENT BY THE GERMAN S.I. [Intelligence Service]

He declares that he was part of the "Gamma" Group of the X Mas Flotilla, only as a driver, and that he had never participated in any other espionage or sabotage organization, German or fascist. On 8 September 1943 he was in La Spezia with the X Mas flotilla whose commander was the frigate Captain Prince BORGHESE. On the following 9th together with sailor VELONA', from his same unit, they loosened up on their own account heading to Pielli (La Spezia) where they were met by Miss PAOLETTI Lois of the place, an acquaintance of theirs. After about a month of staying in Pitelli, the subject left alone, for Laigueglia (Savona), in order to escape capture by the Nazi-fascists, where he certainly met DEL NEGRO Alfonso who he had met in Pitelli. From Laigueglia, in the first ten days of November 1943, the subject went to the Naval Command of Genoa with the hope of being discharged, but there he was again recruited as a driver. For the first two months he continued to wear civilian clothes and then wore the uniform of the petty officer of the X Flotilla MAS. He always stayed at the private home of the petty officer of the navy DE VITTORIO Ludovico (he does not remember the address) also in service at the Naval Command of Genoa.

In February 1944 the subject was transferred to the Navy detachment of Iesolo. After a few days of stay, he obtained a short leave on the 6th to be used in Laigueglia, at his friend DEL NEGRO, mentioned above. Here, thanks to the interest of DEL NEGRO Alfonso, he obtained from the military hospital of Loano (Savona) a convalescent leave on the 24th, at the end of which he returned to the detachment of Iesolo. After a few days he was ordered to Florence for service to collect 600 sweaters from a local company. During the journey with the car (ALFA 500 truck), in Vicenza, the subject met Captain WOLK Eugenio, already his old commander in Sardinia, who asked him if he would like to return to his command. DI CARLUCCIO joined, and as soon as he returned from the service completed in Florence he was transferred to the "Gamma" unit, commanded by the aforementioned Captain WOLK with headquarters in Valdagno (Vicenza). There he was always employed as a driver of the department ave??o [illegible] in delivery of a truck for various services (first a 626 FIAT truck and then a FIAT 1100 van) while the other components of the same department awaited special instructions for the use of assault vehicles, mainly swimming. Of the members of the unit, he recalls the following:

Lieutenant PAOLINI – Lieutenant KALBY – Lieutenant FERRARO – Lieutenant VENTURINI – Lieutenant ZAROTTI – Lieutenant LA CAVA – Second Lieutenant WOLNER – Second Lieutenant MALACARNE – Marshal CAPOZUCCHI – Marshal ARIOLI – Sergeant Major Paratrooper PISCOPELLO- Aldo – Sergeant ALBERTONE – Sergeant MANUNTA – Sergeant TRONVILLE – Sergeant SPEBER – Sergeant DERIN – Sergeant BENDANDI – Sergeant SCARPA – Sergeant DA BOVE – Second Chief VIANELLO – Deputy Chief ARPESELLA Vittorio – Second Chief MAESTRALE Giovanni – Deputy Chief NARDINI – Deputy Chief BERTONCINI – Marine FISHER – Marine MAZZUCCATO – Marine SORGETTI – Marine COBBI – Marine FERRERI Lino – Marine FERRERO-RIGHETTI civilian driver – RINALDI civilian driver, CAON, civilian, guard at the commander's office.

He served with the "Gamma" Group, always with the sole role of driver, from May 1944 until January 1945, when he was admitted to the military hospital in Gavardo (Brescia), where he was diagnosed as suffering from a duodenal ulcer. From there, at the beginning of February 1945, he was sent to the ENT [Ear Nose and Throat] center in Milan to undergo an operation for nasal polyps, which he did not undergo. Towards the end of February of that year, he obtained a 15-day convalescence leave which he used in Valdagno, at a certain Mrs. FABRIS (he does not remember the address) and then returned to the hospital in Gavardo.

He remained there until the end of April 1945 waiting to undergo surgery for appendicitis that he did not undergo because the appropriate room had to move (to another location).

On April 29, 1945, a senior officer of the Republican Navy went to the hospital in Gavardo and communicated that everyone (recoverers and service personnel) were being transferred to the direct dependence of the municipality of Gavardo, because the Germans had asked for surrender.

At the beginning of May 1945, like the other patients in the said hospital, the subject obtained a pass from the local C.L.N. that authorized him to move freely within the district of the municipality. After a few days he went to the C.L.N. in Brescia where, on the back of the pass, he was to join his family in Naples. He reached them in Naples, on May 8, 1945, traveling by makeshift means.

On September 17, 1945, the subject presented himself to the Interrogation Commission of the Royal Navy in Naples and obtained an indefinite leave without pay. To the aforementioned Commission he delivered the certificate issued to him by the C.L.N. of Gavardo.

SPECIAL TRAINING IN ESPIONAGE, SABOTAGE OR SECRET CONNECTIONS:
N. N.

MISSIONS CARRIED OUT AND THE LAST MISSION ASSIGNED:
N.N.

DEPARTMENT FOR WHICH THE AGENT WORKS:
The subject declared that he had been in the service of the "Gamma" group only as a driver, for the transport of food and materials, and that he had been forced to do so to avoid reprisals by the Germans, being unable to reach his family who were beyond the lines.

ANY KNOWLEDGE OF ACTIVITIES INSPIRED BY THE S.I.T. TO BE EXPLAINED AFTER SURRENDER:
N.N.

DATE AND PLACE OF ARREST:
Arrested in Naples by Brigadier GIANNATTASIO Michele
of the Naples C.S. Center, at 7:00 p.m. on October 25, 1945,
near his home.

REASON WHY THE AGENT ACCEPTED THE
MISSION EVIDENCE OF HIS INTENTION TO
COMPLETE THE MISSION:
N.N.

OTHER POINTS OF PARTICULAR INTEREST:
The subject throughout the interrogation proved to be loyal
and sincere, not worried.
No reticence. In some circumstances he significantly strained
his memory to remember the names of people belonging to
the "Gamma" group.
I believe that the statements made by the subject may be true.
Naples, October 26, 1945. (TNA WO204/12452. An
appendix to the report was a list of other X MAS personnel
with details.)

There was then a memo of a telephone conversation dated 30
October.

Telephone conversation Capt Moore/GSI XIII Corps re this
section's letter 704/F/2/1 (Liq) of 29 Oct 45, GSI XIII Corps
Asked whether a representative of G-2, (CI), AFHQ could go
to XIII Corps to discuss the position of X Flotilla MAS
personnel in VENICE estimated at several hundred. XIII
Corps asked for guidance in treatment in view of the fact that
none of them had been given a post-occupational role. I raised
the point that the unsatisfactory aspect of the position was the
fact that members of the ex Fascist Republican forces still at
large and that other security agencies had complained. I asked
XIII Corps to put their difficulties on paper so that the question
could be studied here since the chance of someone from here
visiting XIII Corps was small; it was agreed that this would be
done (Ibid, 30 October 1945).

The outcome of the visit, if it went ahead, was not documented in the X MAS file.

A complication arose when Nichols' letter to SSO(Sy) Med was returned with a note stating that the group was no longer in existence. It had been liquidated and its staff released from duty.

.bject:- X Flotilla Mas.

Main HQ 13 Corps
58/19/I(b)
----

5 Nov 45.

To:-   AC of S G-2(CI), AFHQ.
        (2 copies).

Copy to:- 47 PS Section

Ref your GBI.389.704/F/2/(LIQ) of 29 Oct 45.

1.   The following persons mentioned on the list attached
to your a/q letter are at present employed by the Royal
Navy in VENICE :-

        WOLK,   Eugenio
        MOSCATELLI,   Elrio
        WOLNER,   Roberto
        CASTELLI,   Elyio
        WOLNER,   Enrico
        PAEDO,   Amerigo
        MONTECCHINI,   Ercole
        CAGNOLETTI,   Domenico
        BIANCHINI,   Domenico
        TAMPELLI,   Vito
        STRADI,   Vittorio
        BELLONI,   Angelo
        SCARPA,   Mario
        SPERBER,   Rodolfo

2.   The following persons mentioned on a/q letter have left
for the United States under what are understood to be Naval
arrangements :-

        TADINI,   Camillo
        FREGUGLIA,   Carlo
        BERNI,   Berno
        MERIGHI,   Giulio
        MONTI,   Franco

3.   All the above named persons have been vetted,
interrogated and cleared under arrangements made by Italian
Naval authorities in VENICE and have all been provided by
these authorities with a certificate of security clearance.

                                Brigadier.,
                                General Staff.

FLDF/orh

(TNA WO204/12452)

November 1945

In early November, a General Staff officer sent Nichols a list of those X MAS personnel who had been taken on by the Royal Navy and those sent to the United States.

On 10 November, Colonel Tom Barrat, the Acting Theatre Judge Advocate commented that 'As to whether rewards in the case were paid, British paymasters and Fiscal Director (A) will have to be contacted.'

On 20 November Major C.G. Ratnage acting for Major General DAG stated that 'No record of an award in this case is held by this Branch.' Whether a reward was subsequently paid was undocumented.

On the same day, Colonel Nichols sent the following note to the Main HQ XIII Corps.

Subject: Italian Republican Fascist Organisation.

Reference your 58/16/I(b) of 2 Nov 45.

(1) Attention is called to this HQ's circular GSI.389.701-C of 12 May 45 in para three of which it was stated that in view of changing circumstances the apprehension, interrogation and disposal of wanted enemy agents at large in the then existing 15 A.G. area had become the responsibility mainly of Italian C.S. personnel. In para 4 of the same circular it was also stated that the same principle was to be applied in the existing AFHQ area.

(2) It is in fact agreed that, as requested in para one of your letter under reference, Italian C.S. Personnel be made with responsible for all investigations in connection with subject organisations. A proviso is made to the effect that in the cases of members of Italian and fascist republican organisations such as the X Flot MAS whose names have been circulated in 15 A.G. or AFHQ list of wanted enemy agents and saboteurs C.S. shall refer to this HQ the confirmation of disposal proposed. (Ibid, 20 November 1945)

Also on the same day, 20 November, Nichols sent a copy of the above letter to AFHQ LO IAI [? Liaison Office Italian Army Intelligence] Rome agreeing that 808 C.S. Bn should take over responsibility of handling members of the Italian Republican Fascist organisations and asking them to

...ensure that regional C.S. offices in XIII Corps area are informed of this decision. It is to be noted that when names of members of subject organisations have also been circulated as wanted enemy agents and saboteurs in 15 A.G. and AFHQ lists these cases should be referred through normal C.S. channels and your office to this HQ for confirmation of proposed disposal.

Your attention is invited to the final paragraph of XIII Corps letter from which it appears that CS/FSS liaison in the VENICE area is not as close as it should be. Please investigate the situation and report to this HQ. (Ibid.)

What difficulties there had been between Field Security Officers and their Italian counterparts in Venice was not documented and the report on the investigation was not included in the liquidation file.

On 22 November, 1945, Commander W. N. Baker of the United States Naval Forces, Northwest African Waters. sent the following note stamped SECRET to Colonel Nichols, at Allied Forces Headquarters in Italy. Copies were sent to SENALUSLO [?] (Italy), SSO (Sy) Med. and SCI Unit "Z", Rome.

Subject: 10 Flotilla MAS.
Reference: a) A.C.of S. (G-2) AFHQ sec.ltr. dtd 29 Oct. 1945, same subject.
                b. CNO conf. 1lt to ComNavNAW, dtd. 18 Oct. 1945, same subject.
1. With regard to the status of personnel of 10 Flotilla MAS, subject of reference a), available information is forwarded herewith.
2. Concerning the personnel mentioned in paragraph 1, reference a) as being employed by Allied Naval authorities in Venice, Lt. Cmdr. A. J. MARZULLO, USNR, who has , in conjunction with Lt. Cmdr. Crabb RNVR been working on

underwater experiments with 10 Flotilla MAS personnel in Venice, states that these men are currently working for and under the control of British Naval authorities, and as such do not represent a U.S. Naval commitment. Information as to the present status of this personnel should be requested from British Naval authorities.

3. Concerning the status of the personnel named in paragraph 2 of reference a), paragraph 3 of reference b) is quoted as follows:

"According to their records, four of the Republic and Navy personnel are prisoners of war as defined in near the sub Commission letter NSC/2768 dated 28 June 1945. The remaining enlisted man falls in the status of "Surrendered Enemy Forces", since his date of capture is shown as 1 June 1945. It is anticipated that no attempt will be made to change the status of any of these people in the United States and they will be returned to Italy in the same status they had upon arrival in this country. Lt. Tadini and the four enlisted men working with him have been engaged in demonstrating the Italian SSB and SLC to American Naval authorities. This work is now completed and arrangements are being made to return the personnel to Italy via the first available means. (Ibid.) Captain Moore pencilled on the memo,

'No action at present. We can wait until application, if any, is made to us for disposal instructions. If this does arise, all fire should be disposed of as ordinary PW/SEP/not recalcitrant. (Ibid.)

Lionel 'Buster' Crabb had been the head of Underwater Security in Gibraltar and had several years' experience dealing with X MAS sabotage of Allied shipping. (https://www.visit-andalucia.com/operation-ursa-major-gibraltar/) He and his team of divers had used an early 20th century diving bell to locate and remove limpets and other explosive devices from ships' hulls. 'It consisted of a specially built barge with a rectangular open-bottomed chamber which could be lowered until it was 40 feet [12.19m] below the surface and the divers could then enter it through a shaft leading from the barge.' (Benady, Tito, *The Royal Navy in Gibraltar*, Gibraltar Books, Ltd. 2000, p.173-4) One imagines he would have been interested to acquire the knowledge and expertise of X MAS personnel.

The *Siluro San Bartolomeo*, "San Bartolomeo Torpedo" (SSB) was faster and carried 300 kg of explosives compared to the maximum 250 kg carried by the Siluro a Lenta Corsa, Slow Moving Torpedo (SLC). Three SSB had been constructed by the time the armistice had been signed and Crabb would have wanted to know its details. The Royal Navy and the US Navy would also have been interested in the Italian technology for their own torpedo programmes. (Crociani, Piero; Battistelli, Pier Paolo, *Italian Navy & Air Force Elite Units & Special Forces 1940–45* (illustrated ed.). Bloomsbury Publishing. (2013). p.12)

On the same day, 22 November, Nichols sent the following report to SCI Unit Z in Rome.

Subject: Immunity granted to X MAS personnel.
Reference your JZX-3199 of 16 Oct 45.
1. Please refer to the attached schedules. Individuals against whose name an asterisk appears in Column "A" are those listed, in the enclosure to your letter under reference, as employed by Allied Naval Command, VENICE. Who were "de considerersi discriminate e immune de qualsiasi responsabitieta per l'attivite de essi finora svolta." [to consider themselves discriminated against and immune from any liability for their activities carried out up to now.]
2. With the exception of PITACCO and with the addition of MONTI and BELLONI the actual location of these men is given in columns "B" and "C". According to Main HQ XIII Corps letter 58/19/I(b) of 5 Nov 45 persons whose names are marked with an asterisk in Column "B" were then employed by RN, VENICE; an asterisk in column "C" indicated that the named person had left for the U.S.A.
3. All persons whose named asterisked in columns "B" and "C", according to the XIII Corps letter quoted in para 2

above, all being vetted, interrogated and cleared under arrangements made by Italian Naval authorities in VENICE.

4. Clearance mentioned in para 3 was presumably granted under arrangements made with C.S., and the enclosure to your letter under reference would seem to be the instrument by which that clearance was mentioned (Please refer in this connexion to AFHQ circular GSI.389.701-C of 12 May 45). The only query which arises concerns the word "discriminate" (as quoted in para one above.)/ the sentence would appear to mean that the persons listed were to be considered "discriminated and immune etc…" the normal C.S. meaning of "discriminate "is "unreliable".

5. Authority for the special employment by the R.N. VENICE, of certain X MAS personnel was granted by 15 Army Group. In 15 A G Letter1402/10/I(b) of 29 Jun 45 This HQ was notified that such authority had been given in the case of persons whose names were marked with an asterisk in Column "D". The same letter stated that RN and RIN {Royal Italian Navy] we're making efforts to have those men whose names are marked with an asterisk in column "E" reinstated "As it is proposed to send them to USA in order to act as instructors to U.S. Navy on countering underwater attacks which are expected in the Pacific". A special case was made in that letter of TADINI because of his work for the Partisans and because "he has rendered great service to Allied navies experimental station … in assisting in technical research and instruction".

6. In a letter from the commander USN Forces, N.W. African Waters, to C-in-C, Med., reference AS-2 Serial 004475 of 30 Jun 45, copies to PMG, G-1 and G-2 MTOUSA, request was made for the transfer, in PW status, of the men whose names are asterisked in column

"F" to the USA "to be turned over to the Director of Naval Intelligence, Washington, DC."

7. It is pointed out that policy adopted by this HQ since the surrender has been to regard the pre-surrender activities of X MAS personnel, carried out according to the rules of war, as acts of war. Personnel concerned, therefore, are not now to be regarded as spies and saboteurs but as legitimate members of the enemy's armed forces. Exceptions are made in the case of personnel known to have undertaken espionage work as opposed to legitimate acts of warfare, and in the case of members of the NP and Vega Bn who are classified as "recalcitrant". Furthermore, though technically all former members of X MAS might be treated as enemy PW they would in any case only be given into the custody of the Italians and very shortly be liberated. Conditions prevailing at the time of the surrender enabled great numbers of Italian SEP [Specially Employed Persons] to evade imprisonment and no useful purpose would be served at this stage by attempting to process them as such. It is understood however that under Italian procedure enforce all former members of the Fascist Republican armed forces accountable to the relevant Italian service ministry for their past conduct prior to the surrender.

8. Reference to para 4(a) of your letter, this HQ was not in fact previously consulted as to the special employment of the persons named in the enclosure to your letter; 15A.G. was so informed of and did comment in, certain cases (cf: schedule attached) and may have done so in all cases; if the proposals had been referred to this HQ they would in all cases have been approved. The use of the word "immunity" is somewhat misleading. The sense which it is intended to convey is, however, clearly that the named persons are not to be proceeded against on C.I. grounds

simply because of their membership of X MAS and that even if they had been listed as suspected enemy agents they were not to be interned as such or evacuated as PW so long as they were usefully employed by allied naval authorities in VENICE. The answers to paras 4(b) and 4 (c) of your letter are affirmatives.

SCHEDULE

		A	B	C	D	E	F
	BELLONI Angelo		X		X		
1.	BERNI Berno	X		X	X	X	X
	Bianchini Domenico	X	X		X		
2.	GAGNOLETTI Domenico	X	X		X		
	CASTELLI Elio	X	X		X		
3.	PARDO Amerigo	X	X				
4.	FRAGUGLIA Carlo	X		X	X	X	X
	MONTEXXXINI Ercole	X	X		X		
5.	MONTI Franco			X	X	X	X
	MOSGATELLI Elvio	X	X				
6.	MERIGHI Giulio	X		X	X	X	X
7.	PAMPELLI Vito	X	X		X		
	PITACCO Antonio	X					
	SGARBA Mario	X	X		X		
8.	SPETUENG Rodolfo	X	X		X		
	STRADI Vittorio	X	X				
	TADINI Camillo	X		X	X	X	X
	WOLMER Enrico	X	X		X		
	WOLMER Roberto	X	X				
	WOLK Eugenio	X	X				

Alternative spellings:

1. BERNO Berni - BERNI
2. DELLA GAGNOLETTA
3. BALDO Alberico
4. FRAGGALI - FRAGUGLIA
5. MONTEBIANCO
6. MERIGHI - MERAGHI Julio
7. TAMPELLI
8. SPERBER

--------oOo--------

(Ibid.)

December 1945

In early December, Captain Allen, working for the Brigadier in charge of British Troops in North Africa, sent a letter from No. 211 prisoner of war camp.

SUBJECT: <u>Suspected Italian Political Activities</u>
    <u>CONFIDENTIAL</u>
G.375 6 Dec 45
1. "A number of P.O.W. in this Camp wear a badge of an organisation which they call X Mas. Many conflicting statements are made to me on this subject.
It has been suggested to me that this X Mas was a division of the Italian Army and also that it is an anti-Communist society."
2. Can you please advise this HQ as to the significance of this badge and, in particular, whether it is considered that it should NOT be worn. (TNA WO204/12453)

X Flottiglia MAS badge worn after the Italian armistice
(https://ca.wikipedia.org/wiki/10a_Flotilla_MAS)

On 15 December, Colonel Nichols sent the following note to Allied Headquarters ETNA.

Reference your letter G.375 of 6 Dec 45,

X Flotilla MAS, commonly known as "X MAS" or "Decima MAS" was originally a part of the Italian Navy specialising in assault craft, human torpedoes etc. After the Italian Armistice, those portions of the Italian Navy still remaining in N. ITALY were reformed by the Fascist Republican Government into a unit which was placed under the command of Prince Valerio BORGHESE and to which was given the name, X Flotilla MAS. During 1944 the unit was successively enlarged to include inventory, parachutist and other battalions which were largely used in anti-partisan operations. A unit badge was commonly worn by members of X Flotilla MAS since the Italian Armistice. The significance of the badge is a purely military one and has no intrinsic political character although it is likely that members of X Flotilla MAS who fought with the Republican Fascists will have an anti-communist bias and they can be regarded in general as the "pick" of Fascist Republican manhood. (TNA WO204/12453)

Major Malcom Guist, Operating Commander of No.3. S.C.I. Unit in Milan wrote a report for the War Office. Special Counter Intelligence Units attached to the Allied forces in occupied territory were tasked with locating, apprehending and interrogating Gestapo and Abwehr personnel, their Italian collaborators and stay behind wireless operators, saboteurs and other agents crossing the Allied lines. In collaboration with the carabinieri, the Italian police manned checkpoints 24 hours a day, stopped and checked travel passes. Those they were suspicious of were then interrogated by expert officers in the SCI Unit. Given its importance, copies were sent to the Acting Chiefs of Staff of G-2, the Intelligence Section at Allied Forces HQ; the 5th Army; the 15th Army Group and the IV Corps; the CIC of the HQ of IV Corps; SCI Unit 'S' [Security]; 3 SCI Genoa detachment; 3 SCI Turin detachment; DSM [?Direction de Securité Militaire]; the Italian C/S [?Counter Sabotage] Milan, the M.O. [? Medical Office] and the file.

Subject : 10th MAS Flotilla
1. INTRODUCTION

a) By playing along with the Germans, following the Italian Armistice on the 8th September 1943, the 10th MAS flotilla organisation under Prince BORGHESE retained its independence and enjoyed a large amount of freedom in German occupied Italy.

b) In January 1945, Comandante Mario Rossi, 2nd in charge of the 10th MAS, agreed to work more closely with the Germans than heretofore, and plans were made for an elaborate espionage and sabotage organisation to be recruited entirely from the 10th MAS. ROSSI did NOT, however, inform the Germans that, in the event of a German withdrawal from ITALY, the 10th MAS would stay behind as an independent group to operate against the allies, and that the group would function in order to assist a nationalistic move.

c) To satisfy the Germans' immediate demands ROSSI provided them with some saboteurs (such as LOCATELLI Gino, parachuted in the NAPLES area) Who were to proceed at once into Allied territory.

d) ROSSI, acting on orders from BORGHESE, assembled a special section at MONTOFANO (COMO), as The nucleus of the future Republican Navy espionage organisation, to operate in NORTHERN ITALY after the arrival of the Allies.

e) These men were given courses in sabotage, w/t, and instructed as to how they were first to merge unostentatiously into civilian life as cover for their future activities. Plan of operation was drawn up in triplicate(typed out by seaman Luigi TIRELLI now under arrest. BORGHESE taking one copy, ROSSI another, whilst the fate of the third is unknown.

The first part was a general outline of the plan, the second part referred to the set ups in the various centres and the third give directions on what action was to be undertaken.

2. PENETRATION OF ORGANISATION

a) An Italian Naval Lieutenant, Angelo ZANESSI [? ZANARDI written in pencil], who had been sent into northern Italy on a mission by an Allied organisation, had been in contact with members of the 10th MAS at Verona, and realising that some special movement was afoot, he persuaded Enzo BUCARELLI, an accredited member of 10th MAS, to play a double game, and to keep ZANASSI informed of the course of events. Meanwhile ZANESSI himself, had gained the confidence of some Germans in VERONA, amongst them doing delete being Korvettenkaptein BALZER of the German I M [Intelligence ?] and from him ZANESSI was able to get additional information on the MAS plans.

b) Portable WT sets for the organisation were manufactured by a certain FERRO at   CREMA. By February 1945, men and material were dispatched to the chosen centres from MONTORFANO and in March, false naval release papers were prepared for both officers and men, the date of release being left blank. Civilian cover was assumed, radio mechanics and telegraphist's were given sets and material, and set themselves up as civilian radio experts.

c) About the middle of March, Comandante ROSSI had a long interview with some the S.D. [Sicherheitdienst], and a certain Captain LO CASCIO of the 10th MAS was sent for urgently.   Exact details of the meeting are unknown, but was generally accepted that the Allies would soon occupy northern ITALY and the time for action was near.

d) Meanwhile, Lt. ZANESSI had re-established contact with BUCARELLI and learned that nearly all members of the organisation would be duly established and that Lt. GOZZI in MILAN was administrative officer who would naturally be in possession of important details regarding the group.

e) Events then moved very fast, and only after the entire occupation of ITALY did Lt. ZANESSI have the opportunity to follow up the various leads in order to ascertain if the group was functioning or if the men had disbanded. It was at once clear that every man was at his assigned post - there had been only one desertion (Lt. MAMBELLLI, destined for TURIN had disappeared with all funds entrusted to his care), and the men were awaiting orders from their leader Prince BORGHESE.

3. ROUND-UP OF ORGANISATION

On 19th May 1945, Lt. ZANESSI who was at COMO, Got in touch with an allied security section and offered his services in arresting the MAS stay behinds.

By 24th May, all details on the set-up were known and many of the men were arrested. Appendix 'A' two this report shows the set-up together with results obtained up to date.

b) Interrogation of the arrested persons has revealed that Prince BORGHESE counted on influential friends to assist him in convincing the allies that his organisation was purely a pro Italian movement, and that as such, they constituted NO danger to Allied security. His men would lie low, leading normal lives until called upon when a determined attempt would be made to impose a strong armed nationalist movement on the country.

Prince BORGHESE told them that he would visit southern ITALY very soon after the allies arrived in the north, and meanwhile orders would come from Commandante ROSSI.

c) The various members who have been arrested are at present in the custody of the C.M.L. COMO, and it is recommended that this case should be judged by the Italian authorities.

APPENDIX 'A'   25.5.45

10th MAS STAY-BEHIND ORGANISATION.

Commanding Officer:	BORGHESE Valerio	
H.Q.: -	ROSSI Mario	(Arrested)
Seamen-clerks	MERELLO Carlo	
	DE STANIS	
MILAN		
H.Q.		
COZZI Giuseppe	Administrative officer	(Arrested)
FABERO Piero	Secretary	..
TIRELLI Luigi	Clerk	..
BATTINI Piertullo		
TRANSPORT SECTION (under cover of Societa Italiana Trasporti)		
VENUTA Antonio	C.O.	(Arrested)

SOLARI	Secretary	
DI MAURO	Driver	
BORETTI Virgililo	..	
MALGRANTE	..	
ZUPPIROLLI	..	
PIETRAMALA	..	

PROPAGANDA

CAPRA Mario		(Arrested)

CLOTHING, SHOES etc

CAMERIO Gianpiero	Via dei MILLE 23	(Arrested)

RATIONS

LANGUI Gino	Via FIAMMA 21	(Arrested)
LANGUI Antonio	..	

MEETING PLACE

ROSETTO Sergio	Bar owner, Via RAVIZZA 6	(Arrested)

COVER ADDRESS

BENAZZI Mario	Via ARDITI 8	(Arrested)

W/T Section

TAUSANI Giovanni		(Arrested)
GHIRARDELLI Gino	Piazza SQUADRISMO 10	(Arrested)

BOLOGNA

CUCCIARA Elio	C.O.
BONACCINI Walter	
PANCALDINI Natalino	(Arms and ammunition)
RIZZOLI Carlo	
CENACCHI Augusto	
LUCIANI	W/T

TURIN

MAMBELLI Edmondo	C.O. (deserted)
PARI Elio	
ELLI Ennio	

GENOA

ROSSI Mario	C.O. (Arrested)
PIA Sergio	
BERTUCCI Aldo	..
FRASSONI Carlo	Transport Company (Arrested)

FRASSONI Dionino owners organised by Rossi as cover..
FRASSINO Alessandro   ..

BERGATTA Consalvo
BRUGO
BALDO Remo   (Arrested)
ARDITO Stefano   ..
CINI Ulissa   ..
ANGELI Federico   ..
PRETO Antonio   ..
LIMETTI Giovanni   ..
BORGONOVO
DOGA Pietro
BERGAMO Alessandro
VATTERONI Giuseppe
RIGHETTO Bruno
MANTINI Gieuseppe
LEGOVINI Marcello
ALBERI Italo
CAZZANIGA Emilio
MILESI Vilfrido
OSSI Giovanni
ERCOLINO Antonio
NAPOLITANO Eugenio
NAPOLITANO Raffaele

The Genoa group was destined to commit acts of sabotage in shipyards.

VENICE
CECCACCI Rodolfo (Arrested)
CECCACCI Carlo   .. ?
DEDOLA Angelo
SALGHINI
SAMORANA
BENTI Emilio
VILLA Sergio   (W/T operator)
LEGNANO
CLANCIO Nicola
FERRO Alido
POERU Antonio
BARTOLINI Nando

There was also a list of 22 of the arrested members of the X MAS stay-behind organisation.

FULL DETAILS OF ARRESTED PERSONS

1.ROSSI Mario   Born 24.12.1910 at GENOA. Vice-chief of organisation and O.C. GENOA.

2. FRASSONI Carlo Born 29.11.1916 at GENOA. Manager of a transport company organised by ROSSI as cover for the organisation.

3. FRASSONI Dionino   Born 7.7.1920

4. FRASSONI Alessandro   Born 8,9.1919 at GENOA.

5. LINETTI Giovanni   Born 8.1.1921 at VERBAGNA INTRA.

6, PRETO Antonio   Born 29.11.1911 at COSS (Bolzano)

7. ANGELI Federico Born 6.1.1920 at PORTO VALTRAVAGLIA.

8. BERTUCCI Aldo Born 13.5.1923 at SANTA MARGHERITA.

9. GINI Ulisso   Born 15.6.1921 at BOLOGNA.

10. ARDITO Stefano Born 23.6.1927 at TREVISO.

11. BALDO Remo   Born 11.6.1919 at PADOVA.

12. BATTINI Piertillo   Born 24.11.1920 at RIO SALICETO.

13. GOZZI Giuseppe   Born 3.1.1912 at BOLOGNA

13. CAMPERIO Gianpiero Born 21.3.1914 at MILAN.

15. ELLI Ennie   Born 4.3.1924 at MILAN.

16. VENUTA Antonio   Born 26.6.1910 at PIAZZA ARMERINA (Sicily)

17. BENAZZI Mario Born 20.12.1915 at MILAN.

18. SESSA VINCENZO   Born 10.4.1920 at SALERNO

19. LANGIU Gino Born 21.5.1920 at LECCE.

20. CAPRA Mario   Born 17.6.1910 at MILAN.

21 ROSSETTO Sergio   Born 7.12.1915 at PADOVA.

22. TIRELLI Luigi   Born 10.7.26 at RAPALLO.

Details of other arrested persons NOT yet to hand.

Appendix B was Pancaldi's red account book, extracts from which are included below.

Data	Operazioni	Entrata	Uscita
2 Febbraio	Saldrijo	10000 =	
23 Marzo	"	200.000 =	
"	"	Uffici vari	350 =	
"	"	Lampade		35000 =
"	"	Anticipo Pino		100000 =
"	"	Spese macchina		2130 =
"	"	"		320 =
"	"	Libri cassa		200 =
"	"	Sale permute		25600
"	"	Scarpe 24 paia		31200
"	"	Pini uovo		10000
28 Febbraio	Macchine 500	110.000	
"	"	M.M. 250	36.000	
"	"	Macchine 500		
"	"	M.M. 250		156.000
3 Marzo	Anto Bratta F.lli		
	per pagamento		
	~~...~~	279.120	
5 Marzo	Fondo Spese		
	J.N.I.F.A	234.000	
		879.470 -	360.460

Data	Operazioni	Entrata	Uscita
		879.470	360.450 -
23/3/45	Spese Marcelline	265 -	2.765 =
25/3/45	Carburante a pr...		1350 =
28/3/45	Spese Marchini Milano		1100 =
"	" " Cremona		1000 =
"	" " Modena		500 =
"	Spese ... ghetto		3400 =
"	Anticipo Ceresch.		3800 =
"	" "		12500 =
"	" Rizzoli		12105 =
"	... Pino		...=
"	Spese Pino		226.710 -
"	" "		20.800 -
14/3	Spese ...		660 "
6/4/35	Incassati venduti	107612	
"	venduti	3.075	
"	"	23.250	
		1.014.4..	604.8..

Extracts from Natale Pancaldi's red account book (TNA WO204/12453)

January 1946

Nothing more was reported in the Liquidation file until the end of January 1946 when Lt. Col. D.A. Young, G-2(CI) Section informed GSI(b) HQ No, 3 District that it had been agreed to hand Aniello Di Carluccio over to the Questura 'for disposal as his interrogation report reveals nothing of CI interest.' (Ibid, 29 January 1946)

Conclusion

Although Borghese escaped execution at the hands of the Partisans, he was tried, found guilty and sentenced to twelve years imprisonment for collaborating with the Germans.

On 10 April 1947, almost two years after being arrested and interned, Colonel Nichols ordered the release of the following X MAS men from the CMF "R" Internee Camp: Rino Baldo, Mario Rossi, Elio Cuccharia, Auguste Cenacchi. Natale Pancaldi. Carlo Rizzoli, Walter Bonacini, Mario Bordogna Giovanni Taosani and Albertio Luciani. (TNA WO204/12453) Whether they wrote about their experiences is unknown as is when the other X MAS prisoners were released.

Borghese was released in 1949 for his role in the defence of the Italian homeland against the Yugoslavians in 1945 and the part he played in the defence of Genoa. In 1952, he published his 'wartime' memoirs under the title of *Sea Devils*. An English translation was published in 1954. It made no mention of his collaboration with the Germans after September 1943.

He later entered politics under a pro-fascist and anti-communist banner, gaining the nicknames by some as "The Frog Prince" after the frogmen he commanded, but by most as "The Black Prince". Whether the ex-X MAS men played a role in his political revival is not known. Identified as involved in an attempted far-right coup in December 1970, he fled to Spain where he died a few years later in mysterious circumstances. (https://www.reddit.com/r/ColorizedHistory/comments/6bhd 76/junio_valerio_borghese_nicknamed_the_black_prince/)

Many books and films tell his story but this one has provided the documentary evidence of his stay-behind groups or as he described them, his post-occupational network.

Bibliography

Books

Benady, Tito, *The Royal Navy in Gibraltar*, Gibraltar Books, Ltd. 2000

Borghese, Valerio, *Sea Devils*, Andrew Melrose, 1952

Crociani, Piero; Battistelli, Pier Paolo, *Italian Navy & Air Force Elite Units & Special Forces 1940–45* (illustrated ed.). Bloomsbury Publishing. 2013

O'Connor, Bernard, *Destroying Hitler's R-Netz Volume IV: German-trained stay-behind agents in Italy*, www.lulu.com 2024

O'Connor, Bernard, *Destroying Hitler's R-Netz Volume V: Preventing the Sabotage of Rome*, www.lulu.com 2024

O'Connor, Bernard, *Italy's Mediterranean Sea Devils: Decima Flottiglia MAS 1940 – 1943*, www.lulu.com 2024

Newspapers

Davis, Forrest, 'The Secret History of a Surrender,' *Saturday Evening Post*, 22 September 1945

Documents in the National Archives, Kew

WO202/13000 German Sabotage Organisation

WO204/12452 Liquidation of X Decima MAS

WO204/12453 10th Flotilla MAS [Motoscafo Anti-Sommergibile] and San Marco Regiment [Italian naval sabotage organizations]: stay behind organization

US sources

Hess, Jerry N. (20 March 1967). "Oral History Interview with Stephen J. Spingarn (1)". Harry S. Truman Library & Museum

Websites

https://preview.redd.it/yrljg9ak2vxy.jpg?width=1080&crop=smart&a uto=webp&s=23a534095c9b2ce3ed9d24bd5e1a9fc3fba1bed9

https://www.warhistoryonline.com/instant-articles/scire-italian-royal-navy-sub.html

https://en.wikipedia.org/wiki/Decima_Flottiglia_MAS

https://en.wikipedia.org/wiki/Vittorio_Mocca gatta

https://comandosupremo.com/decima-mas/

http://www.comandosupremo.com/strike-on-alexandria.html
https://historica.fandom.com/wiki/Decima_Flottiglia_MAS#
~text=Decima%20Flottiglia%20Mezzi%20d'Asalto,1943%20dur
ing%20World%20War%20II
https://en.wikipedia.org/wiki/ Decima_Flottiglia_MAS
https://www.dvidshub.net/image/8128570/tactical-ci-italy-nov-1944
https://irp.fas.org/agency/army/cic-wwii.pdf
https://it.topwar.ru/152860-proizvodstvo-otechestvennyh-sredstv-
voennoj-svjazi-v-1940-1945-godah-okonchanie.html
https://ca.wikipedia.org/wiki/10a_Flotilla_MAS
https://www.reddit.com/r/ColorizedHistory/comments/6bhd76/
junio_valerio_borghese_nicknamed_the_black_prince/
https://comocompanion.com/2020/04/27/comos-lake-montorfano-
commandos-contraband-and-the-cia/
https://comocompanion.com/2020/04/27/comos-lake-
montorfano-commandos-contraband-and-the-cia/comment-
page-1/#respond
https://www.congedatifolgore.com/it/a-como-presentato-un-libro-su-
un-nuotatore-paracadutista-della-decima/

Bernard O'Connor's publications on SOE and the Intelligence Services during the Second World War:

RAF Tempsford: Churchill's MOST SECRET Airfield, Amberley Publishing, (2010)
The Courier: Reminiscences of a Female Secret Agent in Wartime France, (Historical faction) www.lulu.com (2010)
The Women of RAF Tempsford: Heroines of Wartime Resistance, Amberley Publishing, (2011)
Churchill and Stalin's Secret Agents: Operation Pickaxe at RAF Tempsford, Fonthill Media, (2011)
'Nobby' Clarke: Churchill's Backroom Boy. www.lulu.com, (2011)
Charles Bovill: WW2 Radio Expert, www.lulu.com, (2011)
Sir Frank Nelson, First Head of the Special Operations Executive, www.lulu.com, (2011)
The Tempsford Academy: Churchill and Roosevelt's Secret Airfield, Fonthill Media, (2012)
Designer: The True Story of Jacqueline Nearne, www.lulu.com, (2012)
Return to Belgium, www.lulu.com (2012)
Return to Holland, www.lulu.com, (2012)
The Bedford Spy School, www.lulu.com (2012)
Old Bedfordians' Secret Operations during World War Two, www.lulu.com (2012)
Henri Déricourt: Double or Triple Agent? (edited), www.lulu.com (2012)
Churchill's School for Saboteurs: Brickendonbury, STS 17, Amberley Publishing, (2013)
Churchill's Most Secret Airfield, Amberley Publishing, (2013)
The COFFEE Party: Soviet Agents Destined for Vienna, www.lulu.com, (2013)
Sabotage in Norway, www.lulu.com (2013)
Sabotage in Denmark, www.lulu.com *(2013)*
Sabotage in Belgium, www.lulu.com (2013)
Sabotage in Holland, www.lulu.com (2013)
Sabotage in France, www.lulu.com (2013)
Agent Rose: The true Story of Eileen Nearne, Britain's Forgotten Wartime Heroine, Amberley Publishing, (2013)
Churchill's Angels: How Britain's Women Secret Agents Changed the Course of the Second World War, Amberley Publishing, (2014)

Elzbieta Zawacka: Polish soldier and courier during World War Two, www.lulu.com, (2014)

'Mike' Andrews: pilot, manager of Liverpool Airport and secret agent, www.lulu.com, (2014)

Blackmail Sabotage, www.lulu.com (2014)

Sabotage in Greece, www.lulu.com (2014)

SOE GROUP B SABOTAGE HANDBOOK, (Introduction), www.lulu.com, (2012)

Agent Fifi and the Honeytrap Spies, Amberley Publishing, (2015)

Agents Françaises, www.lulu.com (2016)

The Spies who came back to the Cold: Iceland's wartime spies, www.lulu.com (2016)

Operation LENA and Hitler's Plans to blow up Britain, Amberley Publishing (2017)

Bletchley Park and the Pigeon Spies, www.lulu.com (2018)

Bletchley Park and the Belgian Pigeon Service, www.lulu.com, (2018)

The BBC and the Pigeon Spies, www.lulu.com (2018)

SOE Heroines: French Section and Free French women agents, Amberley Publishing, (2018)

Operation EBENSBURG: SOE's Austrian 'Bonzos' and the saving of Europe's cultural heritage, www.lulu.com (2018)

Blowing up Iberia: British, German and Italian sabotage against military and economic targets in Spain and Portugal, www.lulu.com (2019)

Blowing up the Rock: German, Italian and Spanish sabotage against Allied targets in Gibraltar, www.lulu.com (2019)

The SOE and NKVD in Afghanistan: Anglo-Soviet Relations during the Second World War, www.lulu.com (2020)

Operation MAMBA: SOE, NKVD and the deterioration in Anglo-Soviet relations during the Second World War, www.lulu.com (2020)

Kurt Konig: German Spy or British Agent, www.lulu.com (2020)

The Little Berkhamsted Spy Ring, www.lulu.com (2020)

Operation DOWNEND: Anti-Nazi Jupp Kappius's subversion and sabotage mission in the Ruhr towards the end of the Second World War, www.lulu.com (2021)

Operations VIVACIOUS and BRANSTON: Anti-Nazi German Jew Robert Baker-Byrne's subversion and sabotage missions in Berlin and Lubeck towards the end of the Second World War, www.lulu.com (2021)

Operation CHAMPAGNE: The changing fortunes of Richard Kuehnel, SOE's first German agent during the Second World War, www.lulu.com (2021)

Internment, Escape and Deportation: Graf Spee and Tacoma seamen in Argentina and Uruguay during the Second World War, Vol. I 1939 – 1942, www.lulu,.com, 2022)

Internment, Escape and Deportation: Graf Spee and Tacoma seamen in Argentina and Uruguay during the Second World War, Vol. II 1943 - 1946, www.lulu,.com, 2022)

SOE in the Marches: The Special Operations Executive in Shropshire and Herefordshire www.lulu.com, (2022)

SOE's BONZOS: Anti-Nazi German prisoners of war trained for sabotage, subversion and assassination missions in Germany before the end of the Second World War, Volume One: 1944, www.lulu.com, (2022)

SOE's BONZOS: Anti-Nazi German prisoners of war trained for sabotage, subversion and assassination missions in Germany before the end of the Second World War, Volume Two: February 1945, www.lulu.com, (2022)

SOE's BONZOS: Anti-Nazi German prisoners of war trained for sabotage, subversion and assassination missions in Germany before the end of the Second World War, Volume Three March 1945, www.lulu.com, (2022)

SOE's BONZOS: Anti-Nazi German prisoners of war trained for sabotage, subversion and assassination missions in Germany before the end of the Second World War, Volume Four: April - May 1945, www.lulu.com, (2022)

SOE's PERIWIG BONZOS: *Anti-Nazi German prisoners of war trained for sabotage and subversion missions in Germany as part of a sophisticated deception scheme* www.lulu.com, (2022)

Blowing up the Danube: British intrigue in the Balkans, www.lulu.com (2022)

The Decline in Anglo-Soviet Relations during the Second World War: The Foreign Office, Secret Intelligence Service and the Special Operations Executive collaboration with the People's Office of Internal Affairs (NKVD), www.lulu.com (2023)

Churchill's Russian Agents in the Second World War, www.lulu.com, (2023)

Operation ETNA: British Infiltration of Soviet Agents into Italy, www.lulu.com (2023) (co-authored with Nicoletta Maggi)

Operazione ETNA: L'infiltrazione britannica di agenti sovietici in Italia, www.lulu.com, (2023) (co-authored with Nicoletta Maggi)

Aimée Corge: One of the last women to be infiltrated into France at the end of the Second World War, www.lulu.com, (2023)

Churchill's Italian Angels: The women who assisted the Special Operations Executive in Italy during the Second World War, www.lulu.com, (2023)

Destroying Hitler's R-Netz: Volume I - Cracking Operation EASTER EGG and Germany's stay-behind agents, www.lulu.com, (2023)

Destroying Hitler's R-Netz: Volume II - Stay-behind agents in France, www.lulu.com, (2023)

Destroying Hitler's R-Netz: Volume III – Stay-behind agents in Belgium, Holland and Denmark, www.lulu.com, (2023)

Destroying Hitler's R-Netz: Volume IV – Stay-behind agents in Italy, www.lulu.com, (2023)

Destroying Hitler's R-Netz: Volume V – Foiling the blowing up of Rome, www.lulu.com, (2023)

Allied Intelligence Services and the Vatican during the Second World War, www.lulu.com, (2024)

Italy's Mediterranean 'Sea Devils': Decima Flottiglia MAS 1940 – 1943, www.lulu.com, (2024)

The Italian X MAS Stay-Behind Organisation: The Black Prince's plans to sabotage the Allies' lines of communication in Italy in 1945, www.lulu.com 2024

www.ingramcontent.com/pod-product-compliance
Lightning Source LLC
Chambersburg PA
CBHW040148010726

47475CB00039B/488

*9 7 8 1 3 2 6 9 6 5 0 4 4 *